MW01382070

Customer Service
A to Z

100 Commonsense Tips for Delivering Great Customer Service

Larry Williams

For information:
 www.LarryWilliams.biz
 775-624-2222
 Larry@LarryWilliams.biz

LCCN: 2010913381
ISBN 978-0-9829611-0-0

Author photo by The Image Gallery©, Reno, Nevada
Cover and interior design and layout by Robert Goodman, Silvercat™, San Diego, California

printed in the United States of America

Contents

Foreword by Dick Clark

Customer Service A to Z is an invaluable piece of work for anybody who is interested in building a business upon good, solid sense. In this day and age, when we are all used to down and dirty sales tactics and hard sales pitches, this book of tips for delivering great customer service will prove to be invaluable.

We often get tied up in the day-to-day difficulties of operating our business and lose track of the common sense basics of service. We all know that service is the basic foundation upon which any business can hope to survive. In this brief but clear-cut guide, Larry Williams has outlined the basic steps that should be taken for success.

Anyone interested in solidifying their own business and building its future can learn from this thoroughly interesting and entertaining piece.

Acknowledgments

There are many people to thank and so much to be grateful for. First and foremost is my faith in God, which has always been a constant. I am very grateful to my parents Sarah and Joe Dietsch for raising me with such traditional values that continue to benefit my life.

There is no greater love I have ever known than that of my family. Being a self-proclaimed workaholic, my wife Selly keeps me continually grounded and reminded of the most important thing of all, family. I love you honey! I have been blessed to have the most incredible kids a guy could ever have. To my daughter Jenny and my son Joey—daddy is so proud of you both and loves you more than anything in this world.

To Kari and Dick Clark, I value our friendship and I am grateful for every moment. Dick, you are such an inspiration to me and I am so honored by your participation in this book. You are the perfect role model, a shining example of class and integrity and so worthy of the praise and love that millions of people have for you. I wish you and Kari many years of great health and happiness.

To Nevada Governor Jim Gibbons, from your courageous service in operation Desert Storm to representing our state as a United States Congressman—you have demonstrated class and dignity at every turn. I admire your leadership and service to our country.

To Jay Conrad Levinson, Leroy Hardy, John Hanson, Kerry L. Miller, Peter Merry, Scott Faver, Bill Chernock,

Lloyd Higuera, Mark Bell, Lynn Jackson and Bill Capodagli...thank you all so much for your friendship, participation and kind words of support.

There are many people who offered technical support and advice for this book. To Robert Goodman at Silvercat, I am grateful for your intellect, patience and honesty. To Mitch Taylor, thank you for your book cover suggestion and friendship. To Charles E. Snyder III, your friendship and extra effort to progress my web presence is so appreciated. To Jeremy Miller, thank you for being such a close friend and advisor. You always put things in great perspective.

I would also like to extend my thanks to: Amy Striebel, Jodi Lee Protopappas, Sharee Dunmore, Amy Levinson, Lisa Merry, Patti Hardy, Julia Jeffers-Peaua, Margie McCaffrey, Kinawati & Antono Wijasa, the Noble family, The Dietsch's—Bob, Rick and family, Aunt Ann Dietsch, Rob & Kari Wigton, Kirby, Shane, Jeff, Susan Bullard, Ken Dworkin, Jodi, Pat and Kara Stone, Kris & Jay Taylor, Deb Struble, Steve West, Robbie Britton, Dr. Drax, Ryan Burger, Mike Buonaccorso, Dan Walsh, Rebecca & Mark Ferrell, Randy Bartlett, my friends in the DJ, radio and wedding industry, Terry Probyn, Jaycee Lee Dugard (and her daughters), Shayna Probyn, Carl Probyn, Terry Gerard, Gary Douglas, Kevin Tokarz, Roger Hoinacki, Jaymee Willison, Michael Lynn and everyone at E!, Juli Jones, Michele Malchow, Tom Entwistle, Cooper Johnson, Paula Leyba, the Ascuaga family, the Pettaway's, the Riekenburg's, the Scott's, the Bell's, the Miller's, my friends, customers, business associates and all who have supported my public appearances both in the past and in the future—my sincere thanks and appreciation!

Finally, God Bless America and the men and women of the United States Military!

Introduction

We live in a fast-paced world. Things change at an alarming rate. What is popular or in fashion today may very well be passé tomorrow. We download entertainment at the push of a button and delete the unwanted just as fast. Runway fashions find their way onto store shelves within days of their debut and thousands of coffee-choice combinations are needed to keep our attention. Technology has made this possible. Computers have dramatically changed the way we get information, shop, and even find the love of our life. Social media have helped many people to enhance their communication skills. Through it all, we adapt and roll with the changes.

These changes, for the most part, have made our lives easier. They help us better navigate our way through life and become more productive and organized. But even while satellite technology can map out the world and cell phones can multi-task better than people, the modern day upgrades we enjoy daily have not replaced good old fashion hard work, dedication, and personal interaction.

These skills can only be obtained through training, effort, and concentrated study. There is no short-cut to success. The skills you learn right now will make you more money, improve your work performance, and help you reach your career goals.

Even if the position you currently hold is a stepping stone to greater things, the important thing is that you acquire skills right now that can progress you through this job as well as the next one. By the time you have arrived at the career you have always wanted, your skill set in customer relations will have been perfected!

Customer Service A to Z is a road map to achieve this goal. When we think A to Z, we tend to think of the alphabet and the full spectrum of letters that make up our language. This book is a collection of ethical standards and characteristics that define customer-employee relations.

So many times people think that delivering great customer service is as easy as smiling and being nice. While these are important, there are so many more things to consider. This book will help you develop a clear understanding of what every customer expects and wants when they do business with you.

The techniques in this book will help you establish a framework for offering the best customer service anywhere! Rooted in traditional principles, these standards have been implemented by the finest companies in the world. This book offers tried and true methods of improvement that have been proven effective with customers and employers alike.

Let's face it: we all want to make more money, work in a great environment, and enjoy what we do for a living. This book will give you tools for connecting with your customers like never before. If you want your customers and your employer to truly value you, you can establish your worth to them by demonstrating top-notch service. This book will help you do just that!

one

100 Commonsense Tips

Time-Honored Techniques to Increase Customer Satisfaction

Personal Appearance

Dress appropriately

The clothes you wear send a message to your customer. Your attire creates an impression that sustains the way people interact with you and hold you in high esteem. Your clothes say a great deal about you. They tell a customer if you are approachable or not. If you are exceptionally well dressed, it can almost guarantee your approachability.

Customers tend to seek out sales associates and employees who dress well. Have you ever been to a supermarket or department store and mistakenly asked someone for a product only to find that the person doesn't work there? If you have, then consider why you asked them. It was likely because their appearance led you to believe that they were an employee.

When you represent an establishment or engage in work within the community, your objective is to build a positive rapport with your customers. Rapport begins with the first point of contact. The attire you choose to wear is saying two things loud and clear to a customer: that you cared enough for them that you took the time to dress appropriately and that you take your vocation and your relationships with your customers seriously.

Unless your employer requests an overly casual dress code, it is far better to overdress in a professional manner than to dress down. Go the unexpected professional mile. Dress in a manner that impresses your customers.

Wear clean and non-wrinkled clothes

In addition to dressing appropriately for work, also be detail-oriented regarding your attire. Customers key into both the message *and* the messenger. By maintaining a clean and non-wrinkled look, you will encourage your customers to focus on what you have to say.

If you wear a uniform, smock, or company-issued outfit, have several and rotate them throughout your work week. Wash and fold your clothing regularly. Your clothing is as much a tool of your trade as a hammer is to a carpenter. If your employer is willing to leave your work attire up to you, don't take advantage of their generosity. Wear clean and non-wrinkled clothes every day. Double check your appearance occasionally throughout the day. Use a lint brush to collect the airborne and contact debris you come in contact with at work.

If ironing your clothes or taking them to a dry-cleaner is not realistic for you, consider wrinkle-free clothes. Much of today's professional wear is made from durable, washable, and wrinkle-free material. Spending a few extra minutes when you are assembling your wardrobe can benefit your reputation and help "iron out" any of your clothing deficiencies.

Keep your hair well-groomed

This seems almost so obvious that you wouldn't think it bears mentioning. The truth is that many workers in the retail environment exhibit a less-than-clean look. It is of special concern when such standards are not maintained where food is served.

While some supervisors may occasionally be relaxed in their discipline, the responsibility truly lies with you, the employee. You should never have to be told to comb your hair and keep it neat. Never put any supervisor in a position where they have to treat you like you were their kid. A good appearance is your responsibility.

You should also refrain from sporting hair styles that might be considered overly unusual. Hair dye, especially when it is applied in an unusual manner, is a common invitation for customers to form a negative perception of you. It can affect your position, employee evaluations, and customer rapport.

This is not to say that your hair must take on a universal, plain vanilla look. But carefully consider the boundaries you might cross if you choose a style, color, or appearance that resembles a cavalier attitude of maintenance. It reflects badly on both you and the business you represent. Let your customer be greeted by a well-groomed employee.

Smell good

Your public persona is influenced in part by how much people find you approachable. Don't do anything that gives your customers a reason to walk away! If you have ever stood next to someone with a foul odor, you know how difficult it can be to excuse yourself from the conversation. You know for sure that you want to leave as soon as the opportunity presents itself. Never let this be an issue that comes up about you at work.

Make sure you smell good. You can use a body spray or powder that has a pleasing scent. With so many things that go on in day-to-day activities, you'll experience any number of conditions where sweat, humidity, and/or outside airborne elements can attach themselves to your clothing, hair, or skin.

Things as simple as a spilled drink or food dropped on your clothing at lunch can be embarrassing. It's a good idea to always have cologne, perfume, or freshening powder available at work, in your purse, or in your car. Like air freshener, your own personal freshness will lighten up the work place. Customers and co-workers alike will breathe a sigh of relief when they are around you.

Body spray or powder can be accessories that accent your wardrobe. Let the scent that surrounds you be a "breath of fresh air" for your customers.

Men—straighten your tie

This is a very simple wardrobe correction that can do wonders for your appearance. You can show every customer you are "on your game" when your tie and other wardrobe essentials are in proper order. When you wear a tie, check several times throughout the day to be sure your tie is straight and neat.

Make a conscience effort to color-match your tie with your shirt and slacks. When you are standing, button your coat. When you are seated, unbutton your coat. A tie clasp adds a stylish look and helps you keep the front and back ends of the tie together.

A shirt and tie or suit is always going to make a better impression than casual wear. You will look better, and your customers will immediately sense that you care enough to dress appropriately. The tie is the ultimate accessory for adding class and distinction.

Customers will not normally compliment you for wearing a tie. But it resonates with them nevertheless. Your tie sends a subliminal message to them. It says that you are ready to assist them in a professional manner.

Don't wear baggy pants

One fashion statement of the hip hop culture has somehow made its way onto the retail scene. It's true that the type of pants you wear will have little to do with your ability to work the sales floor. Still, the number of people who shake their head in disbelief and disgust at this form of "expression" cannot be ignored.

It's not about your freedom to wear baggy pants, but it's about the way other people perceive it. Think of it this way. When you approach a customer and start a conversation, you are hoping to have their undivided attention so they will appreciate your effort, focus on your message, and hopefully, make a sale. The last thing you need to do is distract them by what you are wearing.

Baggy clothing worn by you or anyone else in business can give you a disheveled appearance and affect your ability to make a good impression. For the most part, this is

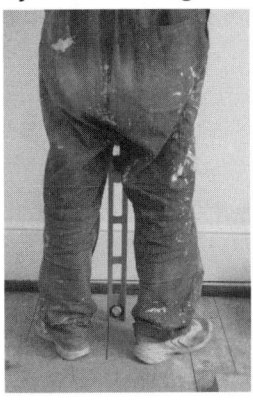

more of a problem for younger people who embrace the hip hop culture. Is that you? If so, then you are one of the people who can benefit from cultivating a more business-like appearance.

Baggy pants can leave customers questioning how seriously you take your job. This is one of the few things in customer service that is a quick and easy fix!

Use breath mints

One thing about offensive breath is this: the person with bad breath is usually unaware that their breath is offensive!  Are you bold enough to tell someone they have bad breath? Most people are unlikely to be that forward. How many times has someone told you that you have bad breath? Probably not very many. Does that mean you rarely have it or that most people are not bold enough to tell you?

Keep breath mints handy and use them many times throughout your day. You are dealing with the public, and you are often just inches away from them. Make sure your breath does not take their focus away from the service you are providing.

Certain foods and drinks can also make your breath smell. Be aware of this when you return to work after lunch or break time. Perhaps the most offensive smell of all is the smell of cigarettes. If you must smoke at lunch time or during your break, have a breath mint at every opportunity.

Bad breath in any social circumstance is a turn off. Improve your customer's experience and increase your approachability by having pleasant smelling breath.

Limit the length of your hair if you're a guy

With a few exceptions, such as mountain and beach communities, long hair and ponytails for men are generally considered social statements of an era long since past. While you'll still see it occasionally in manual labor positions, factories, and warehouse work, long hair is generally frowned upon in most customer service-related fields.

In their push toward professionalism, many modern businesses call for a trimmed look that is commonly regarded as corporate. It is important to maintain a clean cut image, because the way customers perceive your appearance is crucial.

Don't think that emphasizing this is important only at the beginning of your job. Don't let your hair grow longer as your tenure progresses. When an employer hires you, they accept the image that you have demonstrated in your interview. If you were hired with long hair, chances are your employer tolerates it. If long hair was not in style at the time you were hired, maintain a length that your employer will appreciate.

The choice is yours or it is a mandated dress code. Either way, you can impress your customers and employer by maintaining a clean cut image that is consistent with the appearance of your co-workers.

Men—shave before dealing with the public

Facial hair, per se, is not a problem. To the contrary, a trimmed and clean shaven look with no stubble or five o-clock shadow will resonate with your customer.

Just as they will with your clothes, customers will focus on anything unkempt in your appearance. An unshaven look will send the message to your customer that you put little care into your appearance. This invites them to conclude that you don't take yourself seriously and that you don't care about their opinion of you.

Unless your employer bans facial hair, make sure your beard or mustache is well maintained. Few employers will frown on well-groomed facial hair. Make it your policy to maintain neat, manicured facial hair.

Coming in unshaven has little to do with how you perform your craft. Still, don't invite people to conclude that you don't care enough to clean up before coming to work. If someone ever says something like "did you forget to shave today?" they are really telling you, in a subtle way, that your appearance disturbs them.

Remove body piercing

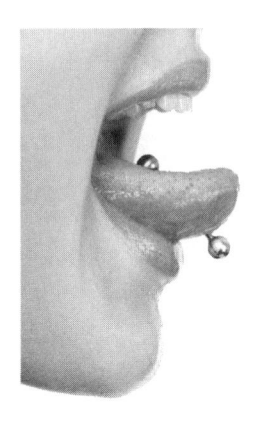

It is not unusual these days to see bodies pierced in the strangest of places. If you have a piercing, especially one in a place that the average person might not expect, consider removing it for the work day. A large proportion of consumers have traditional, conservative values. On the other hand, body piercing is a personal statement of one's individuality. They are standing before you to get service, not to learn about you! They are there to learn of the products and services you offer.

Many employers become frustrated when they hire a person who appears clean cut and business-like but then shows up at work with an unusual piercing that was not evident during the interview. This only sends one message to your employer—that you misrepresented yourself in order to get the job. Don't make this mistake and start your job with a strike against you.

Much like tattoos, body piercings can leave a negative impression with your customer. You want the customer to focus on your ability to serve them, not on some expression that reflects a side of you that should remain personal.

Cover visible tattoos with clothing

This day and age, it is not uncommon to see people with tattoos. They are very popular. However, tattoos are often considered a form of self expression. So ask yourself, would the majority of my customers appreciate looking at my tattoos? People who have very conservative values might be turned off by a tattoo.

Think of a tattoo as a bumper sticker for your body. You don't mind sharing it with the world, but the world might have a different point of view. We all want to be accepted for who we are. But exercising the freedom of self-expression may not always be the best way to warm up a customer to you.

Your workplace environment should be inviting on every level. Visible tattoos may not necessarily conjure up visions of biker gangs the way they would have decades ago. But if they so much as give the customer pause to approach you, they might be best kept covered.

Tattoos can be as off-putting as they are questionable in the eyes of some customers. This may be an unfair stereotype, but it's true! To keep unfavorable opinions from being formed, is may be better for you to refrain from letting the public view your personal form of expression. Remember, the sales process is about them, not about you!

Don't spread germs

Sometimes you are stuck in a close conversation with someone who has a cold or the flu. Your natural reaction is to get away as fast as possible!

We all feel under the weather from time to time. There is a big difference, though, between an annoying sniffle and a full-blown cold. You can usually tell when someone is so sick that they shouldn't be at work interacting with customers. Continual sneezing and coughing, a runny nose, and other symptoms are a huge turn-off to potential customers.

It's more serious with the flu. No customer wants to be anywhere near someone who has the flu. It doesn't matter how much you disguise your symptoms. Subjecting a customer to any contagious illness is irresponsible.

Ask your employer about the appropriate protocol to follow when you are feeling under the weather. Most of the time, your boss will respect your honesty and want you to go home and get some rest. If they are short-handed and you are willing to work, make arrangements that keep you behind-the-scenes and away from customers.

FOLLOW THE GOLDEN RULE

Uphold moral values

Most people are expected to adhere to an understood (though unwritten) moral code of conduct at work. Your behavior is exceedingly important in the way you present your vocation. It truly sets you apart from others who might not take this characteristic seriously.

No matter what profession you are in, you could probably brainstorm a number of things that would be morally unacceptable in your line of work. Follow your instinct on this. There doesn't necessarily have to be a list posted on the lunch room wall in order for you to know what is right. Again, think of it as an unwritten code of moral conduct.

It is also important to steer away from society-driven behaviors that are tolerated in the movies and in music. For example, just because the censors now allow mild curse words on television or in music does not make them okay to use in the workplace.

Resist the temptation to engage in conduct that might be perceived as unacceptable, even if it is harmless. Consider how a customer might react. Any misstep could alienate a customer. Always take the moral high road. It will add greater credibility to the presentation of your craft.

Be humble, not conceited

It is uncomfortable to be around people who are conceited. They often accompany their overconfidence by a boisterous attitude that impresses no one. As you witness this, you may well be forming opinions with each and every word you hear. To be around people who are humble is different and refreshing. These people often respectfully acknowledge and accept a compliment when given. They may act surprised or even slightly bashful. What's most important is the fact that they are gracious, complimentary, and appreciative.

Customers are uncomfortable when they overhear workers glorifying themselves and/or the work they have done. Remember, the customer experience is all about them, the customer. It is your job to accommodate them. Try to graciously accept compliments that come your way. It is not necessary to point out all the great things you do. Let others do that.

Develop the ethical standard to do great things above and beyond the call of duty, without ever becoming self indulgent. When humility is part of your character, others will notice this and respond kindly. Conceit in any form is never respected, welcomed, or pleasant for people to hear! Be humble...not conceded!

Accept criticism graciously

Occasionally, you will encounter customers who are not shy about expressing their opinion. Don't be surprised when this happens. In most circumstances, customers really do mean well. Give them the benefit of the doubt.

All customers have an expectation level. This not only applies to the service, but it also applies to products, company management and policies, the hours of operation, and so on! It is not unusual for customers to express dissatisfaction, offer ideas for improvements, and make suggestions about things they feel should take place.

It is not always easy to step back and hear someone openly criticize something. But part of your responsibility as customer service representatives is to be a good listener, and offer understanding of their dissatisfaction, (and hopefully come up with solutions).

Sometimes, customers will direct their frustration and criticism specifically toward you and the way you take care of them. If this happens, remain calm and hear them out. Their point of view is important. The more you understand their frustration, the better able you will be to address their concerns. Unless they are downright rude, accept the criticism graciously and do your best to resolve the issue.

Respect your marriage

The sports saying, "don't take your eye off the ball!" means don't lose your focus. Customers deserve your undivided attention. There are times when self-serving tendencies and overly friendly behavior can distract from this goal. Your wedding ring (if you have one) is a clear indication of your commitment to your spouse. It represents time-honored traditions that are rich in loyalty and strong moral character.

Flirting is rarely acceptable when business transactions are taking place. This is not to say that it is impossible to meet your significant other while at work. But if either you or your customer is married and wearing a wedding ring, watch out! There is a very good chance you will chip away at your reputation if you engage in dialog that disrespects the integrity of the wedding ring.

Remember that your role is a customer service representative. Remember why that customer is talking with you. Chances are slim that they are shopping for a new spouse! Show some dignity, respect the institution of marriage, and concentrate on business.

Most customers expect you to be socially engaging; however when you turn your back on your integrity, you give customers every reason to distrust your profession and associate it, and you, with unbecoming behavior.

Be a role model

You don't have to be a star athlete or famous celebrity to be a role model. Many ordinary people in the community are looked favorably upon each and every day because of their tremendous contributions to others. You can be a role model because of the things you do that are above and beyond what is expected, and you can be a role model simply because of your caring and responsible work ethic.

Being a model employee is a great first place to start. Once you hone the skills necessary for spectacular customer service, you're poised to establish a reputation that quickly expands through word-of-mouth. People always sing the praise of someone who exhibits model behavior.

Role models are aware of their image. Know your surroundings and anticipate how others might react to you. Be on your best behavior. Be helpful and project a positive image. Strive to improve every aspect of how you present yourself.

Be especially aware of how you interact with your customers. Remember that many people are usually watching you at any given time. Behave in ways that are consistent with being a role model. If you work to achieve it, you will become one!

Treat customers the way you want to be treated

Put yourself in the position of your customer. What are your expectations? Treating others the way you would like to be treated is a time honored tradition that goes all the way back to the Bible, and earlier.

How do you feel when you walk into a big store and no one is there to assist you? Or when you are waiting for assistance and the clerks behind the counter are bantering, laughing, and ignoring your presence? You don't like it, do you?

This commitment to "do unto others" is an important part of great customer service. You don't have to attend a training program to understand how your customers want to be treated. You need only look as far as your own mirror. Keep asking yourself, "How would I like to be treated?"

Treat your customers well and make time for them. You will feel good about yourself, and ensure that the story of the nice person who gives great customer service will be told again and again.

Take responsibility for your shortcomings

"I could have done that better!" You will tell yourself this many times. What worked today, may not work tomorrow. Customer service is an ever-changing activity, one that is continually refined, sometimes daily.

At times, you realize that you could have used better judgment. When this happens, own up to it! Take responsibility for things you might have done better. It's impossible to do everything efficiently. It takes time to hone on-the-job skills.

When you recognize flaws in your work performance, seek out ways to improve. If you need more training in a task, tell your supervisor. Sometimes we make the mistake of saying to ourselves, "yeah, I got this mastered!" only to realize that additional training is necessary. You will never master anything by convincing yourself that "you got it."

Also take responsibility if you engage in unethical behavior or practices. If you are doing something short of professional standards, own up for it and correct it as soon as possible. Always put forth your best effort.

Make each interaction all about the customer

This gets to the very core of exceptional customer service. If you have ever experienced an outstanding employee, you know what a gift it is. The outstanding employee has talent, commitment, integrity, and a variety of other characteristics. It is not easy, and not everyone can do it. While you work hard to perfect, promote, and present your products and services, you also realize that every effort you put forth is for the benefit of your customers. When you make every interaction "all about them," you focus your attention on the most important element of all: customer satisfaction.

Enter into each interaction by trying to communicate that you want the best for the customer. Love your job and love your customers! Find personal satisfaction in every achievement and successful interaction. When you value the accomplishment of helping someone, you want to repeat it with each customer.

Always put the needs of your customer before your own. Always put the praise of your customer before your own. And above all, always attribute your success to them. Because without them, there is no need for you!

Stay true to your principles

Don't compromise what you stand for. Most people have a belief system that is built around God, country, purpose, family, business, or life in general. Morality in business is real and respected.

Years ago, some businesses began to using the symbol known as the Ichthus. It is a religious symbol that resembles a fish. Businesses would place this symbol in their advertisements to show customers that they have Christian values. While this was largely well-received and well-regarded, some businesses, without living up to this standard of morality, used the symbol just to get customers. Most of the time, their true character and lack of morality ended up costing them business.

Never assume that a misguided principle will get you customers. Principles mean far more than just giving lip service to them. They must be demonstrated by your character. Stay true to your principles and allow customers to see that you are passionate about your beliefs. Just don't try to push your beliefs on them.

If you wish to conduct yourself differently because it represents your belief, by all means, continue to do that. People will respect you for staying true to your principles. Remember that your principles represent your character and integrity.

Don't beat yourself up because of an honest mistake

Everyone makes mistakes. You'll have times where, in hindsight, you wish you would have done things differently. Mistakes are part of the learning curve. It's always a good idea to think ahead to help ward off costly mistakes. But sometimes even the best plans go wrong. Unless your mistake is procedural, you'll have several ways to approach most situations. When you are facing one of these multiple choice decisions, chose the one that you feel will work best. If it turns out that you made the wrong call, remember the old adage: "It's better to have tried and failed than to have never tried at all."

Don't compound a mistake. When you make a mistake, own up to it. Denying that you did wrong will only dig yourself a deeper hole. There isn't anyone in business who hasn't messed up at one time or another. Successful business people progress because they pick themselves up, dust themselves off, and get back in the game.

Any time you make a mistake or misjudgment, view it as a learning experience. Take a step back and assess what happened. If you make a mistake, it's okay! You'll progress the next time even better than before!

Show extra kindness to elderly customers

Now and then, it's easy not to consider the feelings of some customers simply because they do not look like the typical customer of a business. Sadly, this happens far too often to elderly customers.

Be extra kind to elderly customers; their contributions may well have made the very job you are fortunate enough to have possible. They have not only paid their dues but, in some cases, they have sacrificed far more than you could ever imagine!

Most of us, including you, enjoy luxuries that most elderly people never had. They deserve your attention and assistance, even if they do not represent the typical demographic of your customer base. Pay close attention to their manners and sincerity. You can learn much from the way they treat others.

Elderly customers are traditional. If you treat them well, they can become your best word-of-mouth advertising. Reward their loyalty with dignity. Treat elderly customers as if they were your own grandmother or grandfather. Your kindness will not only make you feel good, but it will also embellish your efforts to give superior customer service.

Use good judgment

As an employee, you will often be responsible for making decisions. Sometimes you will make these decisions on your own, with no guidance from your employer. Being trusted to make sound decisions is an honor that should not be taken for granted. If your supervisor or employer authorizes you to make an important decision, give it your full attention. Quick decisions and knee jerk reactions will almost never be effective. The way you approach and execute these responsibilities will show your employer that trusting you was not a mistake.

Part of making a good decision is to solicit input from others. Never be afraid to ask others for their advice. When you are facing judgment calls, always consider the possible repercussions your decision might have on others. You may take the safe path and follow the decision-making history of your superiors. After all, if you choose to handle a decision in the same manner your superiors handled it, you will show consistency and be better received.

When you exercise good judgment, you are taking a leadership role. Your superiors will be impressed by your initiative, and your responsibility will be appreciated. When your intentions are in your customers' best interests, your judgments will not often be called into question.

Lead by example

Many people look up to you. It doesn't matter whether they are kids, adults, professionals in business, or senior citizens. Just about every part of your image is being watched by someone. So, set a good example at all times.

Carry yourself in a manner that shows you are a standout employee. Every interaction is an opportunity to improve and build up your reputation. There will always be employees who just go through the motions of their day-to-day routine. Don't be one of them. Be a leader, and set the example that others should strive to achieve.

You also have the ability to change negative perceptions or stereotypes that people might have regarding your profession. Society has stereotyped many professions over the years. When you hear the words "used car salesman," what do you think of? Chances are, you don't want to be like that.

Set a standard of excellence that you demonstrate with every customer interaction. You can set that standard through your actions. Can you imagine the positive reaction if the thousands who saw you do this followed through by practicing the same behavior with each of their customers? Be a standout representative of your profession and lead by example!

Patiently wait for the rewards of your hard work

It takes hard work to achieve success! Everyone's measure of success is different. So, too, is their definition of hard work. Your own measure may be a target rate of pay, a promotion, a title, or line of work.

Set realistic goals for yourself. Many people miscalculate and underestimate what it will take to reach their goals. This is a journey like climbing a high rise building with no elevator. Each floor is a plateau and an accomplishment. Every step you take is necessary to get you to the top of your pay class, your position, or your profession.

Being an exceptional employee will move you to greater heights and monetary rewards with the company. No one in business simple starts on the top rung. Everyone pays their dues. You can too, by hard work and focused attention on your craft.

Be patient. Give yourself a reasonable amount of time to climb the ladder. Your longevity, your employee reviews, and your steady progress in the company is every bit as valuable to your career as the hourly wage or salary you are currently receiving. If you desire greater success, hard work is the only way to get there!

Go above and beyond for customers

There is something to admire about overachievers. You have heard the saying "under promise and over deliver." In layman's terms, do not make promises you can't keep and deliver more than you are expected to.

If you promise a list of things to customers, expect them to hold you to it. If you can offer unexpected amenities, keep these in your back pocket to use at your discretion. Look for ways to deliver an unexpected and unanticipated service. Consider yourself a messenger who has the power to surprise customers with something that will make their day.

Whether it is product advice, complimentary service, just making the customer's visit more accommodating and comfortable, going above and beyond will translate into satisfied customers. Think of how you feel when an employee goes the unexpected extra mile to please you.

As professionals, it is your duty and obligation to deliver service that accommodates your customers. Simply showing up and going through the motions is not enough. Approach every work day with care, excitement, and the commitment to achieve excellence.

WORKING WITH CUSTOMERS

Prepare to meet customers

Have a "game plan" to approach and meet customers. First impressions are very important. Spend time understanding their needs. Learn everything you can about them. Think of this the same way a football team studies film of an upcoming team or the way a boxer carefully examines the strengths and weaknesses of his opponent. Visualize the first greeting and how it might take place. Have a "Plan B" in case any unexpected curve balls come your way. Work this scenario out thoroughly in your head. When the customer arrives, approach them confidently and offer assistance. Let the customer feel that your willingness to help them is genuine.

If you ever travel to Asia and visit one of their shopping malls, you will notice something consistently. There is always at least one person (usually a female) at the front of the store. Her role is to greet customers, answer any questions, and direct them to where they want to go. Customers immediately feel welcomed and their needs are addressed on the spot.

Like the stage performer doing vocal exercises before a performance or an athlete stretching before taking the field, prepare yourself to meet your customers. Be well informed and create a comfortable atmosphere that serves your customers. Preparing before you meet customers will help ensure your encounter is successful.

Be personable

We all enjoy people who make us feel comfortable. When you are personable, you appear more approachable and a pleasure to talk to. Everyone wants to be around individuals who are genuine and sincere.

These qualities are encouraged by many customer service models around the world. Take special notice of companies like Disney, Southwest Airlines, and five-star resort hotels. Study the personalities of people in the hospitality industry. What makes them different? How are they able to establish such great customer service and do it so consistently? The answer is discipline, character, and, above all, a focused effort to be pleasant.

Truly care for your customers; see yourself as someone who can offer them assistance the way no one else can. Welcome them, and invite them to share in the face-to-face experience with you. Let your attitude and your demeanor reassure them that this experience is going to be pleasant and enjoyable.

Customers respond well to someone who is genuine. Be yourself, just as you are—appropriate, informative, and fun to be around. Work hard at being personable. When you firmly establish your personality, you will enjoy great conversations that benefit your career.

Speak eloquently

When you are working with the public, you don't need to have perfect diction. But you do need basic communication skills. Don't worry about being linguistically perfect! Concentrate on speaking clearly and slowly while you annunciate each word. Make a personal connection by looking people squarely in the eye.

If you happen to be on-stage, rehearse each announcement several times before you ever speak into the microphone. Never "dry read" an announcement. Don't be intimidated by the number of people in the audience. They are just regular people who are glad to listen intently to what you have to say.

Work on voice inflections to avoid a monotone delivery. Consider taking a public speaking course or workshop or join a public speaking group. Watch how others speak in public and learn from the way they interact with others. Note what they do and emulate the techniques that are most comfortable and useful.

Above all, relax and focus upon your message. You've rehearsed it! You are familiar with it! Now deliver it! When you pay attention to the way you speak, communicating will become easier and smoother every time. The more proficient you are in your speaking abilities, the more credibility you will have with your customers.

Respect the customer's opinion

You may have heard the saying, "the customer is always right!" It's a time honored tradition in sales. It may not be correct every time. Customers are *not* always right. But treat them as though they are! A more realistic way of phrasing might be, "the customer's opinion always matters!"

Whether the customer is right or not, your obligation is to be informative and to hold their hand through the process. If you respect your customers and approach each interaction as though you valued their opinion, they will feel more comfortable with you and be more willing to work with you.

Listen to what your customers have to say. Not only are their opinions important, but they are also fantastic resources for you to learn from. Your ability to understand where they are coming from is vital in your efforts to assist them and steer them in the right direction.

By treating others with respect, you are telling them that you value them. It's like anything else in life. When you value someone, you appreciate them and hold them in high regard. So, value your customers. You need them as much as they need you, if not more. Respect their opinions and they will respect you!

Recognize and acknowledge

As you get to know your customers, you might discover some things about them that are worthy of your praise. If you learn of a birthday, marriage, anniversary, graduation, or other recent milestone, offer your congratulations. It's a quick and easy way to instantly put a smile on their face. Look for things that can allow you to offer sincere validation of their interests as well. Acknowledgements can mean a great deal to people. Don't be afraid to ask questions, just so long as your questions take on the form of "small talk." Don't let customers perceive you as someone who is prying into their personal life.

For example, if a customer is wearing a New York Yankees ball cap or other piece of clothing, break the ice by acknowledging them as a fan. Tell them of your favorite team. You will be surprised where a conversation like this might lead. You might even learn of their graduation from college, recent marriage, or other achievement.

The key here is to know when to back-off and get back to business. Always get to know your customers and support their achievements and interests. When you can genuinely "warm up" a customer, you will have crossed the first hurdle in public relations.

Earn your gratuity

There are several circumstances, especially in the hospitality and similar industries, where tips are customary and expected. In some cases, it is factored into the final cost of the service. Many employees are hired at a reduced hourly rate, so the gratuities provide the majority of their revenue source.

Nevertheless, even when tips are customary, a tip must be earned. Customers generally consider a tip optional for someone who meets or exceeds expectations. It is a give-and-take, not an entitlement! The longer you work in customer service, the better you will understand the connection between exceptional customer service and gratuities.

There are many employee positions where no established gratuity policy exists. If your position is one where tips are not expected, don't anticipate one. Expecting a tip may subconsciously affect the manner in which you treat customers. Never make the mistake of assuming that tips entitle customers to better customer service.

Customer service is taking care of the customers' needs. The customer's economic class or willingness to tip should never matter. Work hard to earn the praise of your customers. If that praise happens to come in the form of a gratuity, consider it an unexpected benefit for a job well done.

Appreciate every compliment

Compliments fuel your passion. Every compliment is like a brick that slowly, over many years, builds your dream home. Without compliments, the dream never becomes reality. With them is a feeling of pride and knowledge that each brick has a purpose that contributes to the overall structure.

The next time someone gives you a compliment, listen intently. You will be able to measure the sincerity in their voice and see it in their eyes. Some forms of gratitude are so heartfelt that you can't help but feel overjoyed. Most people in our society don't give compliments freely throughout their day. When they do, appreciate the effort and the choice of words used.

But never let compliments go to your head. Let them be the fuel that drives your passion to give good customer service. Enjoy the moment, but not for too long. Get right back to work and let your achievement inspire even more focused efforts for customer service.

Appreciate every compliment that comes your way. Accept compliments graciously and work hard to deserve the trust and praise of your customers.

The right music makes a difference

To realize how much music can enhance the customer's overall experience, put yourself in their shoes. The tricky thing about music is that there are many styles and so many people with different tastes. Many styles annoy people, too. If the decision is up to you, look for a neutral balance.

Have you ever been in a restaurant, retail store, mall, or other place of business where the piped in music was either too loud or didn't match the surroundings? This can annoy customers. If you were in Tower Records or Planet Hollywood, for example, you would probably expect to hear an upbeat blend of popular music. But if you were in an Italian restaurant or children's clothing store, you might find that same music doesn't fit the overall experience.

One rule to follow is to take yourself completely out of the equation. Don't select music simply because you like it. Select a musical style that the majority of your customers are going to appreciate.

Always best to put their preferences before yours and play it safe with neutral music. If you control the music, pay special attention to the style and volume on the floor. It should always be a mood setter, not a deal breaker.

Don't talk too much

When you are dealing with customers, be as good a listener as you are a talker. Conversation is a two way street, not a one lane road. Approach each customer with the intention to share the conversation equally.

You may well find yourself leading much of the conversation at first. But as things develop, find ways to engage your customers in conversation. Make them feel like active participants, not just spectators. The more they share, the more opportunity you have to engage them in conversation and better address their needs.

In sales consultations, exercise good judgment and don't get into dialog that is awkward or uncomfortable for anyone. Nobody wants to be around someone who talks too much. If you find yourself doing all the blabbing, ask your customer a question. Allow them the opportunity to contribute to the conversation.

When you are speaking before a large group, don't make unrehearsed or unprepared announcements. If you must ad-lib, be direct and to the point without elaborating. People will always respond more favorably to someone who doesn't talk too much and respects the contributions of others.

Always smile

When you smile before you talk, the tone of your voice will reflect it. Try it before you answer your telephone. Practice it before you make an announcement to a group of people. As a customer service representative, your smile can be another acknowledgement of how approachable you are.

Music is the universal language, and a smile is the universal symbol of peace. If a smile can break down barriers of hostility in foreign lands where the language is not understood, just think of what it can do with customers. Make a smile the first thing you give each customer. They might eventually experience your expertise, advice, direction, and helpful manner, but they will first get your smile.

Practice your welcome line with a smile. Then recite it without a smile. Do you see the difference? Customers will be drawn to you when you greet them with a smile. This validates that you really want to help them and aren't there just because your boss told you to be there.

You have probably heard the saying, "when you smile, the whole world smiles with you." You would be hard pressed to find any other single act that improves public relations for a business more so than a smile.

Educate customers without sounding preachy

You may find yourself in a position to offer information and help a customer make a decision. Be careful not to overstep by sounding too authoritative. While it's true that you are perceived as the expert, the manner in which you deliver the message makes a big difference.

There is a fine line between somebody who is well versed and someone who knows it all. Choose your words carefully. You can destroy a meeting, a sales consultation, or an interview by sounding too smug in your certainty. If you sound like your position is absolute or dismiss an opposing viewpoint out of hand, your advice will generally be poorly received.

Use phrases such as; "it has been my experience" or "I recently learned through careful examination and training." This implies that you possess a level of expertise that is based on something concrete, such as your experience or your training.

Remember, customers need direction. They do perceive you as the expert. However, they have thoughts and opinions of their own too. Find the delicate balance of being informative without being preachy!

Offer support for customer requests

It is not unusual for customers to offer a suggestion or request. Consider this suggestion as a contribution. When they offer their ideas, show them you appreciate their taking the time to do it. Then, address their request.

It is difficult for some people to come right out and offer a suggestion. Most people simply accept the policy, procedure, or practice and move on. Recognize that they had the fortitude to follow through with something that is important to them. As you hear the opinions of your customers, use it as an opportunity to retool your efforts to serve them.

Do not criticize or dismiss the request or suggestion. That is demeaning and implies that their opinion does not matter. Watch your body language, head movements, and facial expressions. These can also communicate an impression that you are not interested in what they have to say.

Here are three rules to follow: Listen—Acknowledge—Act. Listen intently to what they have to say; acknowledge their opinion; promise to pass their suggestion along to the appropriate party. When you treat requests and suggestions in this manner, you will develop a greater appreciation for what they feel when they approach you. Unless they use a rude and inappropriate tone, they are telling you that they want to help.

Give the impression that you enjoy your job

When you seem confident and friendly, it affects everyone around you. It's kind of cool to realize that you have the power to control the mood and environment of where you work! What could be better than that? People love being around others who have a positive attitude.

Nothing is more disturbing to a customer than to be around someone who seems uninterested in their job. Sometimes, a customer will even hear an employee verbally express dissatisfaction with their job, a co-worker, a product, or the employer. This is one of the most egregious errors of judgment an employee can commit!

Whether you see your job as a stepping stone to bigger things or are unhappy with some aspect of your employment, never let your customer know! For years, this has been a problem with organized pickets and employee demonstrations over labor and wage disputes. While they might keep up the pressure on the employer and make employees feel better, in the long run they distort perceptions of the business and alienate even the most loyal customers.

Let your customers see that you enjoy your job. It tells them you are happy to be around them. You will find that people react to you with more respect and courtesy. Remember, everybody likes to be around people who enjoy their work.

Always be truthful with customers

At times, you will have to undertake the difficult task of explaining something unpleasant to a customer. You may be tempted to take the "easy" choice of deception. Don't. Choose honesty!

Customers can see right through someone who is deceptive. Just ask a politician. From small town government to the White House, we have all seen politicians wrestle with being honest under pressure. They learn the hard way that their reputation would be far better served if they are forthcoming from the very beginning.

Lying to customers is a bad practice. It does damage to your reputation, because customers almost always find out they have been lied to. Then they blame you. When you have to explain something difficult to a customer, trust that the customer can handle the truth a lot better than a lie.

Customers have already placed their trust in you. If you violate that trust, you risk your entire relationship with those customers. Though they may not always agree with your decision, most customers will respect the integrity and character you demonstrate when you are up-front. Honesty truly is the best policy.

If a customer chooses someone else, wish them well

Sometimes you'll discover that a customer decided to do business with someone else. This can be difficult to accept. Your first reaction may be to make sure that they will be sorry for not choosing you.

But there is something else at play here. Your character and genuine concern for them will constantly remind them that you have class. This may someday get you a future customer.

Customers will remember the person who wished them well more fondly than the person who doesn't. Just because someone didn't become your customer the first time around doesn't mean they will never become your customer unless you engaged them in unconstructive dialog, challenged them about their decision, or gave them some other offense.

You will not win over every customer who comes along. If you do not get their business, wish them well. If you know and like the product, service, or person they have chosen over you, by all means, affirm that their choice was a good one.

Maintain a family-oriented atmosphere

Sometimes your customers will come in with their family, and you will be dealing with people of all ages. Your place of business should show that you are aware of what is appropriate for all ages to see and hear. Avoid any sort of dialog, interaction, or body language that is inappropriate or in bad taste.

Have guidelines for dealing with customers of all ages. As a professional, every word you say should be appropriate for anyone of any age to hear. Think of your workplace as a family-oriented community event, a supermarket, or an amusement park. How do *their* employees act around guests of all ages?

Or consider some of the role models in the public eye. You can learn a great deal by comparing the style and class of one celebrity role model to the tabloid front-page exploits of another. Pattern your image after role models who have class and character.

Pay attention to well-established and well-defined customer service models in successful businesses. Your own success at creating a family-oriented atmosphere will be well received and help create the word-of-mouth that enables you to stand out from other businesses.

Be confident

When you project confidence, you tell your customer that they don't have to worry about your intelligence or your ability to serve them. This reassures a customer that the buying experience will likely be a pleasant one. Customers expect you to be knowledgeable. If you stepped into their business, wouldn't you expect them to be just as knowledgeable? Learn all there is to know about the products and services you represent. Try to anticipate the questions your customers might have and know how best to answer them confidently.

Your confidence should extend far beyond your product knowledge. Confidence is a great icebreaker when you first deal with customers. Smile, be accessible, and don't wait for the customer to approach you. Extend a greeting and offer your assistance right away. This shows a confidence that will reassure your customer.

Your confidence should be genuine and humble. Be careful not to give the impression of over-confidence. Over-confidence can be misinterpreted as conceit. Be confident in your abilities in a manner that doesn't look like you are convinced of your superiority.

Address your customers' fears

You may occasionally encounter customers who are apprehensive about a product or service. If you notice this, bring it up and address their fears head on.

In the wedding industry, for example, customers often worry about DJs who might exercise poor ethics or self-proclaimed wedding coordinators who have no formal training or certification. Responsible members of these professions are acutely aware of this fear and will address it up-front with a customer.

Say a product or service you offer has received some bad press. It is completely acceptable to address this with customers and to let them know about changes or improvements that have been made. The same is true for service "after the sale". This can be very important to customers, but until you bring it up, they may not even know you will take care of them.

Most customers are reluctant to express their fears. Part of your job is to sense or anticipate them. If you can nail down what worries them, you can address it and restore their peace of mind.

Take Care of Business

Embrace training

Any time you start a new position with a company, there is bound to be some training involved. You may find the training repetitious or unnecessary. Still, give your employer the benefit of the doubt, and understand that all training programs and procedures are intended to make your job easier. No matter how long you have been on the job, you can always benefit from more training. You need not look any further than actors, actresses, comedians, and/or athletes to understand why. The very best in the world still train aggressively. When you see great baseball players working with a batting coach, it's not because the coach is better than they are. It's because the coaches are trained to notice areas of improvement that neither the average person nor the star player can see. Your employer likely possesses similar tips for success.

Most employers are prepared to train their employees to be well-versed in the areas necessary to represent the company well. Most will offer a well-defined training program for you to follow. This will likely detail all important aspects of customer service, product knowledge, etiquette, and cooperative team efforts.

Embrace the training that your employer offers you. Remember that refresher courses and employee evaluations allow you to fine-tune areas of improvement. The more seriously you embrace the training offered by your employer, the more likely they will recognize you and your accomplishments.

Don't overstep your authority

Some of us take such ownership of our job position that we become domineering and throw our weight around. To "pull rank" on another employee or to openly take charge of a situation that is outside the scope of your authority can cause great damage to your reputation.

In 1981, when then President Ronald Reagan survived an assassination attempt, the first words anxious Americans heard were from Secretary of State Alexander Haig, who stepped up to the podium and declared "I am in control here!" His poor choice of words gave out an impression of misguided authority and caused serious problems for Secretary Haig's reputation from which, sadly, he never recovered. More than forty years of service to his country is still forgotten because of those five unfortunate words.

This example shows how one person (perhaps you or a co-worker) can get caught up in a well-intended need to take charge, especially when you feel your contribution might be best for the situation at hand. If workplace situations require immediate attention beyond your job responsibility, consult others and make informed decisions. Don't pull rank!

Solving problems can be a rewarding experience. But it must be realized through contribution and the proper chain of command. Tread softly on matters that are better addressed by someone else who is in the proper position of authority.

Limit personal activities that can affect your work

When you accept a paid position, you agree to respect the integrity of that position. By virtue of your acceptance, you agree to arrive promptly, work hard, stay focused, and dedicate yourself fully to the day's work. Spending the evening before your workday partying or involving yourself in strenuous physical activity before work can affect your workday routine. To let that happen sends a message that you do not value your position.

Your days off are certainly your time to spend as you please. However, when you are at work, you have the obligation to respect the responsibilities of the position you were hired for. Think of this as conditioning. Your body and mind should be conditioned and focused upon work. This physical and mental preparation should be on-going, even in your off hours.

Think of athletes training for a marathon. They don't just pay attention when they are actively training. When they are away from the track or weight room, they are careful not to do anything that might disrupt their next training day. The same is true for concert pianists. You don't see them pounding nails on a construction site on their days off. Their hands are their vocation and livelihood. They give much forethought and care to keep their tools in perfect operating condition.

Your ability to perform your job requires a regiment of discipline that honors the commitment to your vocation. Carefully examine your "off the clock" activities and consider if they might contribute to a counter-productive work day. If they do, then change your routine!

Safeguard company secrets

Any time you train with a new employer, you will learn things that are proprietary or expected to be kept on the "down low." This means they are not to be shared with others. Think of this like a chess game. Just like one player doesn't want to let his opponent know his next move, a business never wants to tip its hand by revealing its strategy.

Respect this confidentiality so that a competitive edge can be maintained. If a competing company should learn of the techniques, procedures, and intellectual property that makes your business run more smoothly, the spiraling effects of compromising this information can affect sales, demand, and even your job.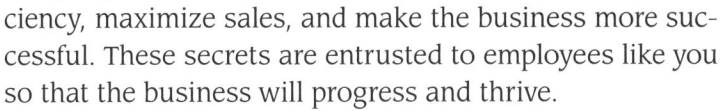

The bottom line is: *don't share company secrets with anyone!* The information you are privy to is designed to improve efficiency, maximize sales, and make the business more successful. These secrets are entrusted to employees like you so that the business will progress and thrive.

Whether they are printed or written, procedural or structural, or related to suppliers customers, these secrets must remain safe with you. In some cases, letting the cat out of the bag can ruin a business. Keeping the secrets will gain greater respect with your employer.

Neatly arrange your work area

Take extra time to arrange your work area in a manner that is safe and organized. A customer is more likely to stay longer, shop more, and comfortably relax in a business environment that is clean and good-looking. Make tidiness an on-going routine.

If you work in retail, straighten the product and front-face the merchandise. Double check that all merchandise is in its proper location. If  you work in the health profession or food service, be familiar with laws that are enforced by state and local inspectors. If you see potentially hazardous obstacles, it is your responsibility as a company representative to safeguard customers from harm. Notify the appropriate person or department for assistance.

Most customers are not bold enough to point out or comment on an unorganized or dirty work area. They simply look around and then leave. You might assume that they did not find what they were looking for when, in fact, they may have thought the unkempt appearance was indicative of the way you do business.

Never wait for a supervisor to tell you to straighten up the area. If your work area is neat and nicely arranged, no one will notice because this is precisely how it should look. However, if it is not, everyone will notice!

Make new employees feel included

Every new-hire employee approaches day one with an excited nervousness about the experience that is about to begin. We have all been there! The experience itself can be as overwhelming as the position. But one universal condition can make this experience more enjoyable. That is the cooperative treatment of the new hire by co-workers!

Welcome new hires and make them feel part of the team. Show them around, assist them at every opportunity, and reassure them that your first day was overwhelming and challenging, too. Your reassurance will put their mind at ease and allow them to concentrate on the new policies, training procedures, and circumstances they are sure to face. Camaraderie will help foster an environment that allows business operations to work like a fine-tuned machine.

Remember how you felt that very first day by putting yourself in the position of the new hire. Show them respect, courtesy, and positive reinforcement. Let them know you truly value them. Find unique ways to make their work day fun and enjoyable. Look into the future. You will realize how pleasant and beneficial it is when your new colleague comes to work each day with a great attitude.

A harmonious work place is a pleasure for everyone involved. It takes effort on everybody's part to make this happen. But the advantages and benefits that come from creating a working environment that is fun, rewarding, and enjoyable make the effort worthwhile.

Be punctual

Allow yourself enough time to plan for any emergency or delay that can come up while you are traveling to work or an appointment. When you accept a job, you are promising to be available for specific hours of the day. You are agreeing, through a verbal or written contract, that you will arrive on time and be ready to perform your job.

There is a saying in business: "It is better to be one hour early than one minute late!" Remember this aphorism and practice it to the letter. Nothing is more frustrating to an employer than an employee who is continually late.

When you are habitually tardy, you convey the message to your employer that you consider being on time to be nothing more than a formality. What many employees fail to realize is the tremendous burden this places upon their employers. Arriving to work late often affects payroll, shift changes, timely store openings, and relationships with fellow employees.

"Acts of God" and unforeseen circumstances always can occur. But when you prepare for the unexpected and allow yourself plenty of time, you can make a positive, lasting impression on many individuals. If you are on time, you will also experience a minimum of workday stress.

Drive responsibly

Does the way you drive affect your job performance? After all, it *is* part of your job performance! When you are behind the wheel of a company vehicle, you are not on a break! Your judgment and road etiquette, while you are at work, can reflect well or badly on your company and, therefore, on your employment.

If you find yourself on the road for business—especially when you are driving a company vehicle—recognize that your behavior on the road is more visible than your behavior in a stationary location. For example, consider how many people can see you when you are in your vehicle.

"Rules of the road" are a common denominator in all business. Nearly all employers consider them to be as important as their other policies and procedures. If you drive as part of your job responsibilities, remember that your employer should never have to tell you to pay attention to speed limits and drive responsibly.

Your road etiquette while you are working is every bit as important as your responsible behavior in the work place. Operating a motor vehicle demands the same attention as operating a piece of heavy machinery. It requires concentration and focus. Safety is always paramount in the business vehicle. Drive safely!

Don't let personal problems affect your work

Find a common balance between your personal life and your time at work. It may not be easy to do. It takes conditioning and discipline. Stay focused at work and refrain from bringing personal issues with you to the work place. Employers and supervisors can relate to the struggles of balancing family life and career. It is not easy for anyone. However, work is work and your time spent on the job needs to be focused on the tasks of your job.

Don't take personal calls on the job. If you have personal matters to take care of, do it on your break time. Let your spouse and children know to call you only for emergencies. They are your support team. You need their help to make this work. They must understand the importance of your work and your need to avoid interruptions that could affect your activities and focus.

It may be difficult, but don't let personal problems affect your performance. Make an effort to limit or eliminate interruptions caused by personal issues. This takes a deliberate effort to do, but your customers deserve your undivided attention.

Avoid co-worker confrontations

Work place rivalry has been around forever. It can develop out of many different factors, including jealousy, seniority, and job performance. However, personality conflicts can be avoided if you can take the high road and turn away from confrontations.

Strong personalities and stubbornness are often involved in these conflicts. Be careful about getting into a dialog that calls someone out or puts them down. Most employers have protocols in place for reporting, evaluating, and documenting work place complaints. Follow the protocols, not the passion.

Especially in large companies, groups of individuals may team up like a wolf pack against a co-worker they don't like. There is nothing productive from behavior like this. The best way to avoid these conflicts is to head them off before they become issues.

When you sink to the level of putting down co-workers, you are tainting people's perception of you. Don't play that game. It will get you nowhere. Don't let your opinions about a co-worker drive you to put someone down. Don't make it about you. "If you don't have anything nice to say, don't say anything at all."

Be a team player

Sports teams understand what a team effort is. Every person on the team has a job to do. Executing their jobs properly can make the difference between winning and losing the game. Many companies encourage team building. Embrace this team mentality. It fosters unity and camaraderie. If group projects are undertaken, by all means participate. If you do this effectively, you will see favorable employee reviews and receive special consideration for advancement. Work to interact with co-workers on a regular basis, whether it is required or not. Word will travel fast when you go beyond your job description to assist someone else. This doesn't mean you take on someone else's work load. But, when you see a co-worker who is struggling with a task, chip in and help. If a colleague is stressed because of excess merchandise that needs to be stocked on the shelves, lend a hand. Or, if a co-worker is running late during a shift change, offer to stay until they arrive.

Doing small good deeds can and will have a lasting positive effect on the other members of your team. It helps build team loyalty, and your employer will reward you for going the extra mile.

Correct transaction errors immediately

It doesn't happen often, but you will make transaction errors. Everyone does. But when it happens, it deserves your immediate attention. If you have overcharged a customer, billed them incorrectly, or returned the wrong change, correct the error as soon as possible. Locate the customer and if you can't do that, inform your supervisor of the error.

What if somebody dropped a wad of bills while standing in front of you at the grocery checkout? Would you pick the bills up and place them in your pocket? Or would you kindly let the person know they have just dropped something? If you do the right thing, you are not alone.

When customers purchase products or services from you, they are saying they trust you. Gaining their trust is your first step in forging a solid relationship with them. This, in turn, can lead to return business and word-of-mouth referrals. But, if you remain silent about a transaction error, you will run the risk of damaging this positive relationship. Don't take the chance of a customer calling you to point out a mistake you didn't try to fix!

Value your customers and always look out for them. They will appreciate you and the job you do more when you correct transaction errors as soon as you discover them.

Appreciate the responsibilities of your superiors

This is not to suggest that you worship the ground they walk on. But at the very least, consider the responsibility they have as supervisors. Most experience a greater level of stress and pressure to perform their duties. They have a boss to whom they must answer, just as you do.

In just about any workplace, the higher you travel up the ladder, the more you have to deal with, be responsible for, and answer to. Put yourself in their shoes. Their job may not be an easy one!

Understanding what they're going through may explain their actions and their reasons for making decisions that affect you. And who knows? Someday what you observe may come in handy if you ever accept a supervisory position yourself.

The pressures of authority may be tremendous and impossible for subordinates to understand. Think of it this way: the more elevated the position, the more it needs your understanding and cooperation. Whenever possible, give your supervisors the benefit of the doubt, and remember that they are under pressure and expected to perform just like you are!

Know your company's business affiliations

If the business you work for is a member of an organization, ask your employer for specific details about this group. Why? Because it might just be the perfect tool to close a sale!

Your company's involvement in a union, guild, or trade organization is marketable to customers. Proudly display certificates and plaques in high traffic areas. You have seen reception areas, showrooms, medical offices, and work areas where these status symbols offer credibility and peace-of-mind to customers.

Learn about these affiliations and have a general knowledge of them and the benefit they offer your customers. Use this information to build confidence, appreciation, or close a sale. In customer service, which in many ways is tied directly to sales, it is important to utilize every tool of information at your disposal to build consumer confidence.

Most of today's unions, guilds, and organizations create a solid foundation for businesses to grow, prosper, and compete. Customers are reassured by this involvement that your company is sound. They will never know about it, however, unless you bring it to their attention.

Be aware of client-friendly policies in your contract

Where contracts are used, some provisions will favor your customer. While a business must safeguard its interests contractually, its contracts cannot be one-sided. The contract should also contain policies or provisions that are in the customer's interest. Identify these and bring them to your customer's attention.

Customers are naturally fearful and uneasy about signing contracts. Often, they enter into these transactions apprehensively. Whether the contract is for the purchase of a home, an automobile, or services, your customers will rely on your guidance to see them through this transaction. Misleading them would be irresponsible.

Transparency is an important word these days. It means you offer a full accounting of the way you operate your business. When it comes to contracts, you need to be as forthcoming as possible. Show that you respect the interest of both your company and your customer. A contract should never benefit one side more than the other. It is there so both sides are protected.

In a contract, policies and provisions protect the interests of both buyer and seller. Learn what these provisions are in your contracts, and point them out to your customers. Let them know that you are a responsible partner to do business with.

Take care of company equipment

In your day-to-day routine, you may well use equipment your employer provided to help you carry out your duties. This equipment is important and costly. Treat this company equipment with care.

How would you treat it if you owned it? Think of your vehicle, cell phone, or any other of your valuable possessions. Would you appreciate it if one of your friends didn't treat it with care? Probably not!

Let everyone see that you handle company equipment carefully. Your employer and co-workers will noticed and appreciated it. You'll reduce the chance that you'll be accountable for broken equipment when you can demonstrate a record of caring for and maintaining it.

Equipment maintenance, repair, and replacement are all costly expenses that come right out of the pocket of your employer and its bottom line. Increased company expenses generally means reduced revenue that can be spent on employees. Be a responsible care taker of the company equipment that your employer has supplied. It's in your best interest.

Keep your office clean

A clean office sends the message to a client that you are well organized. A dirty or cluttered office can give the impression that you don't care what people think about your business. If you take your organizational skills seriously, you will send the right message to your customers. You can't predict when you will invite a customer to step into your office. Not all office visits are by appointment only. At times you will need to invite a client or customer into your office on the spur of the moment. These are the times when you'll wish you had a clean office.

How often have you dropped in on someone announced? Did you see an unexpected side of them? Was it favorable? Surprise office visits do occur more often than you might think. If you are prepared, you'll be better able to impress your customers positively.

Be prepared. Keep your office clean and looking good. Discipline yourself to make this part of your workday routine. You shouldn't have to fumble around a cluttered office, especially with a customer looking on. It can mean the difference between looking organized and looking careless and sloppy.

Stay healthy

Most paid positions require some amount of physical activity, stamina, and concentration. If only for this reason, it is important to take care of yourself. Pay attention to what is most demanding about your job. For example, if you are on your feet all day, strengthen your ankles and legs with exercise.

Don't forget vitamins and a healthy diet. Both enhance your overall well being. Simple activities such as walking can do as much for you physically as it can mentally. Staying active, even for only a few minutes per day, can clear your mind and relieve the stress of the workplace.

Also pay attention to your visual health. For those who are at a desk all day, the constant focus on a computer monitor can lead to headaches, poor concentration, and irritability. This is why breaks are so important. Take time every so often to step away, clear your mind, and change your environment. This does wonders for your outlook when are in the middle of a busy workday schedule.

Pay special attention to your health and the benefits it has for your day-to-day activities. Make smart health habits part of your routine. Working can take a toll on both your body and mind. By making a conscience effort to improve your health, you will positively affect your life and improve your job performance.

Contribute to a consistent chain of service

If you are in the retail or hospitality industry, your customer may have come to see you by way of several other people. You may be just one person in a long list of people who have serviced their needs. The customer may have spoken to someone else first on the telephone, at the information counter, or on the sales floor and then made their way to your station. Recognize the contribution others made to keep the customer happy. Any departure from this positive chain of service could ruin what everyone has worked so hard to achieve.

If you happen to be one of the people a customer met early in their visit, realize that your service, attitude, and decorum was instrumental for your colleagues down the road. Never send along an upset customer or pawn them off on someone else in your company. You have to assist them appropriately at every link in this service chain.

Make your customer service exemplary and consistent at every point. A single failure in the chain can hurt the sale and damage the reputation of your business. A consistent chain of service is an important feature of customer satisfaction.

Embrace change in the workplace

Almost every business is a constantly evolving and changing process. Besides the ever-changing array of products and services, on-going developments always alter the way businesses are marketed and advertised.

Your day-to-day routine is one place where change occurs often. Never get so married to an idea, routine, sales pitch, or policy that you blind yourself to other possibilities, scenarios, and options. Closing your mind hampers your ability to move ahead.

Imagine you work at a radio station. For decades, a common practice at radio stations has been to change the music format abruptly. One week your favorite Adult Contemporary station could turn into a Country Music station. While this might lose loyal customers, the decision was probably made to increase the listening audience. Remarkably, station personnel roll with the changes. On-air personalities, sales staff, and office crew understand that these changes can happen, and they should not affect the delivery of service.

The next time your employer changes things, embrace it! This will broaden your abilities and help you reach more of your potential. Remember the Sheryl Crow song, "A change will do you good!"

Follow protocols and chains-of-command

Whatever business you are in, you'll always need to consult with others when important decisions need to be made. These situations often require quick thinking and a calm demeanor. Strive to learn the proper protocol or chain-of-command so you can maintain a positive customer experience.

Consider each situation to be one that requires a timely response and professional etiquette. Follow the appropriate chain-of-command. Be flexible enough to adjust the way you respond according to the importance of the situation.

You are like a police officer directing traffic. You need a 360 degree view of the road. You need to know where people are and what direction they are going. You need to anticipate when a driver is approaching the intersection too fast. You need to correct for large buses and emergency vehicles that require a travel priority. While you are doing all that, you need to be fair, organized, and ready to make split second decisions.

Discuss scenarios with your employer and learn what is expected of you. You will make great decisions if you clearly understand the proper protocol and chain-of-command.

Adhere to the policies where you do business

How would you feel if someone tracked mud into your house and rudely demanded something from you? You probably wouldn't like it. Whether you work in a fixed business location or on the road, the minute you set foot in someone else's environment you become a guest in their house!

This is especially applicable for service men and women who often travel throughout the community. Just because you have been asked to perform services on location does not mean you have been given the green light to make yourself at home.

Do not take liberties with businesses or customers who have welcomed you through their door. They have opened up their business or home to you. Meet this with grace and appreciation. And remember that they have policies that may be different from yours. Respect their wishes just as you would like them to respect yours.

Always cooperate with others to create an atmosphere that reflects your professionalism and respectful qualities. Follow their policies and respect the environment they have created.

Offer helpful ideas

Everybody looks at things differently. You can be a "fresh set of eyes" for your employer. When you suggest improvements, you tell your superiors that you care and want to contribute to their success.

In the old days, a business would have a suggestion box, usually located in the back room. It was a simple box with a slit at the top for workers to drop in suggestions. Nowadays, such a box seems rather primitive. Today, workers use the chain-of-command and offer suggestion directly to their supervisor.

When you prepare a suggestion, follow these simple guidelines. Offer a suggestion for increasing efficiency and productivity. If the idea also saves the company money, you're even better off. Don't criticize the way things are currently done. Finally, make sure your suggestion improves more than just your position.

Most employers appreciate input from their employees. Be a proactive member of the team. Look for ways to maximize efficiency and improve business operations. Any sincere suggestions will have a positive effect on your reputation.

Good Ideas

Work hard to establish rapport

Establishing a rapport takes a lot of discipline. You will have to work hard to maintain a consistent focus day after day to achieve this goal. It begins by being personable and approachable.

When you are approachable and make people feel included, they will be comfortable doing business with you. Customers always respond more favorably when they feel welcomed, appreciated, and valued. Work hard to make them feel that way at every level of your business. This will help you achieve a great reputation and customer rapport.

Continually revisit every facet of your company or your business. Remember that you are only as good as your weakest link. Regardless of all your positive achievements, your reputation can be hampered or damaged by one person, incident, or disparaging remark. Find a way to monitor your efficiency.

When you give the customer a feeling of ease and peace of mind, you will have established a positive, progressive rapport that your customers will talk about favorably.

Network

When you want to know your friends better, you spend more time with them. When you want to expand your business knowledge and explore new avenues, you network. Surrounding yourself with like-minded individuals is a great way to discover new opportunities. Think about joining organizations or groups in your community that meet weekly or monthly. Take  every opportunity to network and share ideas. You will open up many doors for the future. You never stop learning, and you never stop growing!

In addition to face-to-face meetings with colleagues, you can take advantage of all the on-line resources for your industry. These provide many ways to address new ideas, revisit old ones, and develop new skills that can enhance your business. Set a goal for yourself to contact two or three new people each week. Meet with them and follow-up either through social media, telephone or, better yet, in-person contacts. Nurture these new-found friendships.

When you take the time to meet with other business professionals, you increase your opportunities to gain knowledge, insight, and respect. Networking is one of the best educational tools for advancing your efforts in business. Don't just work...network!

Send out "thank you" cards

Thank you cards serve three important purposes. They are great to receive, they show appreciation, and they reaffirm to the customer that their decision to do business with you was a good one.

When you consider sending a thank you card, keep in mind a couple of things. It is best to write the card yourself. Cards are more meaningful to the recipient when they are hand-written. It shows that you made an effort to personally take the time to write. It is also important to address them properly by name and to offer a salutation that is appropriate and meaningful.

A thank you card does not need to be long in order to be effective. It does not have to go into great detail. Consider a general mention of your interaction, thank them, and express your appreciation that they took the time to see you. Give careful thought to the words you use. Remember, less is usually more!

In sales, it is always important to keep communication open. Let your customers know how much you appreciate them, and assure them that their decision to do business with you was the right one. Send them a thank you card.

Keep your composure

Working with the public brings new challenges and new opportunities every day. Occasionally these new challenges can become frustrating. When you have to go with "plan B," roll with it and keep your composure! Part of your unwritten job responsibility is to keep things flowing smoothly.

Often, these circumstances are not within our control. They might be caused by a customer, a co-worker, a scheduling conflict, a computer malfunction, a product shipment, or any number of other parts of the equation. Whatever might stress you out throughout the day, stay composed and find the best way to manage the situation you are in.

Rely on teamwork and your experience. If you are faced with a challenge that exceeds your capabilities, don't be afraid to request help from a co-worker or supervisor. There is nothing wrong with telling a customer you do not know the answer to a question. It's more important to let them know that you will find an answer that addresses their concern.

There is something to admire in those who stay cool under pressure. Your ability to stay composed during difficult situations will reduce your stress and provide a smoother transition through turbulent times.

Publicly support your country

Even though politics is a very touchy subject for some, patriotism is still alive and well. Offering support for the country where you live and work is always well received, as long as you exercise good judgment when you do it.

Those who remember the tragedy of 911 also remember the public display of patriotism that followed. For months on end, American flags were attached to vehicles, community fundraisers gained overwhelming contributions, television and radio publicly supported the military, and first responders were hailed as heroes. Nearly everywhere you looked, Americans proudly displayed their support of their country and the red, white, and blue.

In this country, bumper stickers that support the local police and fire departments rarely provoke controversy. The same is true when people wear American flag pins, tie tacks, or yellow ribbons. Symbols that reflect patriotism and/or history are usually perceived very well. They can even add favorably to your image.

Consider the manner in which you deliver the message. You do not want to appear overly obsessed with your point. But an occasional soft display of support of the country where you live and work is most always in good taste.

Approach humor cautiously

Do you consider yourself funny? If so, that's great! There is no better feeling than to make people feel happy. But introducing humor at work might be something altogether different. You always risk offending someone.

It is difficult to gauge a customer's tolerance of humor. Before you introduce humor into the conversation, give it careful consideration. We all want to be personable. But there is a fine line that can be crossed if you don't exercise perfect timing. What's funny to you might be insulting or inappropriate to someone else.

Know your customer well. It is usually better to let the customers initiate the joking. Let *them* take the conversation to a humorous place. Consider yourself as their audience. Even if a dialogue or a comeback is called for, do it carefully and appropriately. Again, let them introduce and control the direction of the conversation.

Part of customer service is being personable and establishing a rapport with your customer. Whenever you consider introducing a comedic element into your job, do it appropriately and stay within the expectations of your customers.

Fix negative personality traits

While someone's unique personality can be refreshing, it can also be very uncomfortable when a customer has to endure any of your personal traits that are better reserved for your closest friends. In customer service, it is important to find a balance that expresses your personality in a traditional and expected fashion.

Customers do enjoy casual conversations with someone who has a welcoming personality. They also want the experience to flow smoothly and effortlessly. If your personality provides this objective, then by all means use it to your advantage.

However, unique mannerisms that appear lackadaisical or even different may work against you. Customers can be turned off by something as simple as an over-exaggerated laugh, stare, question, or story. Your body movements, posture, and opinions can be very misinterpreted if you presented them in a manner that is unbecoming of a customer service representative. Be personable without being too personal.

When you deal with customers, keep things conversational, comfortable, and accommodating. Let the positive side of your personality shine through and get rid of those self-expressive traits and habits that can be misunderstood or uncomfortable.

Limit your cell phone use

Chances are you own a cell phone and use it to communicate while you are out and about in the community. Cell phones are convenient on a personal level and useful for those who travel on business.

However, in spite of the cell phone's advantages, it also has disadvantages that can affect the way a customer perceives you. If you are talking or text messaging on a cell phone in clear view of customers, you can give the impression that you are more involved with your telephone conversation than your job. Be careful you don't do that!

Especially in the retail and hospitality industries, cell phone use should be prohibited, just as they would be in the classroom or in a house of worship. Annoying or loud ring tones can also disrupt a business environment. Anything that takes focus away from the customer's experience should be used only with carefully considered discretion.

Discuss the appropriate use of cell phones with your employer. You may find that cell phones are not even permitted on the sales floor or around customers. Better yet, take the initiative and don't use your cell phone at all. Let your employers know that your cell phone is off when you are around customers and watch how much more value they place on you as an employee.

Put a professional message on your voice mail

Many customer prospects are lost simply because the service representative has left a non-business sounding message on your voice mail. Whether you run a home-based business, a retail store, or another business where a telephone is used, customers expect to hear a business professional on your end of the line.

If a business has a boring, generic, or plain vanilla message, customers will not only be unsure about leaving a message; they will also question the wisdom of doing business with you. Customers want to be reassured that they have reached a professional business where they can get expert, professional service.

Put yourself in their shoes. You call a law firm, a retail store, or a wedding photographer, and all you hear is "Hey, I'm not here right now. Leave your name and number after the beep!" What do you think after you hear a message like that? Chances are you dial other numbers until you hear a real person or a business-like message.

Getting voice mail is annoying enough. Getting a message that doesn't reflect a professional business is a slam-dunk negative experience that will cost you business.

Always have a back-up plan

The unexpected happens far more often than you might think, so plan for the unexpected. Contingency plans are like the "fire drills" you remember from elementary school as a child. You practice them and work out different scenarios in preparation for Plan-B.

Pay attention to the back-up plans your employer already has in place. If you work in retail, chances are there are several contingency plans for ringing up transactions, covering shifts, ordering, bookkeeping, and stocking the back room.

In a service-related industry, customers do not care about the equipment necessary to complete the task. They care only that the task is completed and the service is rendered. It is your responsibility to have contingency plans in place. If your equipment fails, you have backup equipment readily available to minimize the disruption of service.

Whether you deal with curve balls customers throw at you, changing conditions in the service industry, or the multitude of scenarios that can play themselves out, you need a fully developed back-up plan ready for implementation.

Offer options

Customers appreciate knowing the options that are available to them. You can communicate with them verbally, via literature, or even by displaying products.  Whether their purchases are motivated by price, quality, workmanship, service, or demand, most consumers will appreciate knowing the many options available to them.

Customers will trust you to be well-informed and knowledgeable about your products and services. They assume that you have been instructed, educated, or trained to do your job well. Don't try to fake your way through this. If you do not have the information your customer needs, find someone who does.

Give your customers options. This could include giving them detailed consumer information about a product or even letting them know how a similar product might be better for their needs. You can do this only by taking it upon yourself to know the products and services sold by your business and its suppliers.

Offer sound options to your customers. They will appreciate your helpfulness and remember the person who assisted them to make the best decision.

Give back to your community

Public service in any form is a worthy activity. People always recognize and appreciate those who roll up their shirt sleeves and help their community. The act of giving back and participating in community oriented events, fundraisers, and awareness campaigns is not only good for your soul, but it will also impress onlookers.

There are many ways you can offer your products or give of your time to help the community. Become involved in local organizations and events. When you are approached for donations or support, know the protocol of your company. If the request needs to be handled by a particular individual, follow the chain of command to the proper person.

If you can fill a need through your talent and expertise, do it. Be humble, and consider that your involvement is a small contribution that will contribute to the success of the event. If your company sponsors a little league team, the Special Olympics, or some other popular cause, share it with your customers. Let them know that by supporting your business, they are also supporting a cause that means so much to you and your co-workers.

Community involvement is a powerful affirmation of your character. The positive recognition you receive, not to mention the goodwill and referrals, will add greatly to your reputation.

Choose quality over quantity

Everyone wants their business to grow and succeed. However, when you sacrifice quality in an effort to increase production (or efficiency, or some other goal), your customer and your reputation usually wind up paying the consequences.

Beware of cost-cutting measures intended to increase production. Take personal responsibility for the quality of your product and services. If standards are not being met or quality is being sacrificed, talk with your superiors. The odds are that they will appreciate your personal concern if you share it sincerely.

Proactively inspect your products and services from time to time to make sure it meets your quality standards. Show your customers that you take it seriously. They will respond with purchases and praise for you and your product or service.

Your customers will be as consistent in their loyalty as your product or service is consistent in quality. They will speak well of your business and your attention to detail. Slow and managed growth that maintains the integrity of your offerings is far better than taking on too much in an effort to increase production.

Look busy even if you're not

Customers who see how hard you work will appreciate you and the business you represent. It's show time, and you're on stage! Always look involved. Interact with customers, co-workers, products and equipment. Stay constantly busy! Don't look too relaxed when you walk around. Always send a message that your product or service is available because of the hard work that you constantly put into maintaining it. Don't let customers ever question your dedication to your vocation.

Just because the product is sitting on the shelf or the service is being delivered, don't think you can sit back and let it sell itself. If you have a lackadaisical approach to what you do, you will give the impression that you are not interested in the work.

While modern technology helps us manage our time more efficiently, it also frees up a great amount of time. Find ways to look involved and interested in your work. Think of yourself as an actor. Play the role of an involved employee. Don't ever give the impression to a customer that your job is so easy that anyone can do it!

Strive for perfection

Always work to improve your efficiency. Just like a car working on all cylinders, you need to remain focused on doing things productively. This means you need to educate yourself about things you have not yet mastered.

The football team wins the game by executing everything it has been trained to do. Players know and show more passion and drive than their opponents. That doesn't mean they are perfect. What it does mean is that they continually monitor and adjust their skills and techniques.

In a football game, there is a winner and a loser. When you deal with customers, you have either a satisfied customer or one who is not yet satisfied. They may not be dissatisfied, unless they are completely unhappy with how they were treated. But they may simply not be sold yet on the idea of doing business with you.

Always strive to make customers happy and satisfied. You will never be perfect at that. Perfecting your craft and customer interactions will be something you'll do throughout your career. The reward for your effort will be customer satisfaction and a good reputation.

Check the accuracy of advertisements

Double-check the accuracy of all the advertisements you use at work. It is not unusual for errors to fall through the cracks. Sale dates, out-of-stock items, typos, inaccurate information, all can unintentionally mislead a customer. If you discover anything inaccurate, bring it to the attention of your supervisor immediately.

Advertising is not limited to what is in print. It also includes what you say! Word-of-mouth advertising is also very important. Badmouthing the competition only makes you look less professional. Nothing is to be gained from stooping down to the level of juvenile jousting.

An advertisement is something to inform a customer. It is not a "shot across the bow" intended to incite a response from your competitors. When you run advertising that is untrue or unbelievable, you create a reason for customers to question your honesty and integrity and the good intentions of your efforts.

Whether it is printed advertising, in-store point-of-sale displays, or word-of-mouth recommendations, periodically check the accuracy of your advertisements to ensure they reflect the products or services you offer.

Use careful dialog with unsatisfied customers

Whenever you work with customers, there is a possibility you will encounter someone with an attitude. A customer might approach you and expect you to resolve a problem immediately. They might have a real problem with a product, service, return, or the transaction itself, but they could also be having a bad day.

People will usually speak their mind and talk to you in the same manner they talk to friends. Often they are frustrated. They won't hold back their emotions. Think before you answer, and exercise restraint.

The very job you have can influence the nature of the interaction. For example, customers at an auto parts store come in because they have a problem with their vehicle. They think of their visit as an inconvenience. The same is true for people at the Department of Motor Vehicles or wherever there is a long line to receive service. Those who work a hotel front desk often meet customers who are tired and cranky from a long day of travel.

Not all your customer interactions will produce happy customers. If you ever confront an unsatisfied customer, smile, take a deep breath, and find a way to help them without losing your cool.

BAD IDEAS

Don't invite friends to work

While it might seem innocent enough, most supervisors frown on socializing at work. Several things at play here could damage your reputation. For starters, it is simply not within your authority to grant permission or a special invitation for people to visit your place of work. You would be hard pressed to find an employer who would encourage this sort of invitation.

The presence of a friend can contribute to a social atmosphere in the workplace. Most employers expect you to concentrate on work and not conversations with friends. This, in turn, would give your superiors cause to question your priorities and dedication.

Liability issues also come up when friends assist you or travel in work areas not designed for untrained and uninvited people. If your friend gets injured as a result of their extended stay on the premises, your employer may have to deal with legal complications, insurance problems, and worker's compensation insurance investigations. Any of these consequences can jeopardize your job security.

Unless it is authorized and/or encouraged, don't invite friends to work. Your job requires your undivided attention. Any distraction, regardless of how innocent it may be, can seriously affect your reputation and tenure.

Don't discuss politics

Certain topics should always be approached with caution. Politics is one of them. In just about any social circle, you have a fifty-fifty chance of alienating someone. Those are not good odds.

There are always at least two sides to every political issue. In the United States, these sides usually revolve around a liberal or conservative viewpoint. Both sides can be passionate about their stance. In fact, it is nearly impossible these days for the average person to discuss an opposing viewpoint without being passionate.

Politics can be compared to interpreting the bible. If you ask ten ministers to interpret a bible passage, you are likely to get ten different interpretations. The same is true for politics. Everyone has a viewpoint, but most of the time, when politics is discussed, few opinions change. Your worldly viewpoint is unlikely to offer any sort of earth shattering revelation that suddenly gains the respect of those hearing it. Therefore, keep your opinions to yourself!

Is expressing an opinion about politics worth the damage that can be caused to your overall reputation? Think of it this way: when you talk politics, you give your customers an opportunity to vote you out of office!

Avoid chauvinism

It is one thing to have an outgoing personality. But it is something else altogether to flaunt an overconfidence that implies a superior mindset. This is especially true in dealings with members of the opposite sex. Nothing is more annoying than someone who thinks gender arrogance is cool or some kind of sport.

Be especially sensitive to how you speak about others. Whether you're talking about a co-worker, friend, relative, or customer, avoid sharing stories or opinions that might be misconstrued. Denigrating someone of the opposite sex or implying that their abilities or intelligence is inferior will hurt your reputation, cost you business, and jeopardize your tenure in your job.

Chauvinistic behavior, even when done in jest, can be considered "sexual harassment." Not only can it cost you dearly with your employer, but it can even lead you into civil and criminal prosecution.

Such behavior will almost never be tolerated. So don't treat women poorly or speak to them in a manner that can be considered demeaning or condescending.

Never drink on the job

You would be very hard pressed to find any business or industry that allows employees to drink alcohol on the job. Unfortunately, a small proportion of employees still believe it is acceptable to drink while at work.

As professionals, you have responsibilities to your customers. Consuming alcoholic beverages while at work does nothing to help you fulfill these responsibilities. It is self-serving behavior that contributes nothing to the workplace.

Don't drink even at lunch! The alcohol in a drink or two may be noticed on your breath when you return to work. Bragging about your drinking escapades or hangovers is also a *faux pas.* It only amplifies any negative impression of you and your habits. Don't glorify something that could be misperceived!

Drinking on the job puts you, the employee, in an indefensible position. There is no way to talk your way out of it. It's wrong, and no employer will cut you any slack for it. You cannot come up with any good excuse for drinking in the work environment. Drinking and making excuses will do your reputation far more harm than good. Don't drink and work!

Smoke only discretely

People who smoke often find it difficult to go long periods of time without lighting up. As a result of new laws around the country, there are fewer places than ever before where smoking in public is permissible. Even if smoking is allowed where you work, most customers do not smoke and do not like it when you do.

The effects of second-hand smoke are just as much a concern to non-smokers, especially now that serious forms of cancer have been linked to second-hand smoke. Non-smoking customers know they don't have to put up with the situation. Is it possible to lose customers if you smoke on the job? You bet! Walking away is very easy for customers to do!

If you are a smoker, find out when and where you can light up discretely. Take your cigarette break at a time that does not disrupt your work and in a place where people who see you are not likely to associate your smoking and your job. End your break prematurely if you have to. And don't forget to carry breath mints!

Give some thought to using gum, patches, or other prescribed medications to curb the urge to smoke. If you are a smoker, watch your timing. Condition yourself in your off hours to go long periods of work time without smoking.

Never let customers see you yawn

A yawn is one of the most embarrassing things a customer can see. When a customer sees you yawning, their first thought is that you are bored or tired. And let's face it—few things are worse than looking like a person who is bored with his or her job.

Get plenty of sleep. If caffeinated drinks or coffee do the trick, by all means enjoy them (but not in front of your customer!). If you must yawn, cover your mouth with your hand. Better yet, turn around or dip your head behind a counter.

Certain work conditions will make your eyes heavy, especially long meetings, video presentations, and dark environments. Look for ways to stimulate your senses and keep you alert. If chewing gum is allowed and keeps you from yawning, then go for it. If you can enjoy a cup of coffee during the meeting, ask yourself if you want it with cream and sugar or just black.

Do whatever it takes to keep from being seen yawning. You may never lose a customer because of it, but yawning certainly won't impress your customers.

Keep negative comments to yourself

If you hear or see something bad or wrong at work, don't add your own negative spin to it. Stay positive and address it with something constructive. This is especially true if the situation involves a co-worker. Don't criticize your fellow employees, especially in front of customers, which can leave a tainted impression of you and of the business. Hearing you or any other employee make negative comments, regardless of the reason why, is a real turn-off to a customer. It certainly doesn't help you make their experience enjoyable.

In addition to speaking negatively, also be aware of your body actions and facial expressions. They can say just as much as the words coming out of your mouth. Rolling your eyes, shaking your head, or making a quick exit can create an impression of indifference—or worse.

The best way to fix a negative situation is to do something constructive or positive. If you see something that is simply not right, roll up your shirtsleeves and help solve it. Negative comments will almost always reflect badly on you. Sometimes they do more damage than the thing you are complaining about.

Never let a customer hear you curse

This can be a disaster for your reputation. We have all done it at one time or another. In attempts to develop a relationship with our customers, it's easy to let your guard down and slip in a mild curse word to get everyone on the same level.

This is not to say you should avoid friendly conversation. To the contrary, a big part of building a rapport is making the customer feel at ease. One way to do this is to engage in pleasant, relaxing, and welcoming conversation. But, when you let a casually spoken curse word enter your dialogue, you make building a favorable reputation more difficult. Off-color language sends a message that your people skills are less than professional.

The same is true even when customers overhear you use curse words in a separate conversation. It doesn't matter whether these words are directed toward fellow employees or someone you are talking with on the telephone. The fact that customers hear such language will still damage your reputation and credibility.

A single curse word, uttered intentionally or inadvertently, can hamper your goal of maintaining a professional edge customers look up to and respect. Protect that edge and tone by never letting a customer hear from a side of you that usually comes out on a night with your close friends.

Never cancel a customer without good reason

This behavior happens more often than you might think. It is often done by employees who think they have a better opportunity to advance their financial position. When customers have chosen to do business with you, they have also committed themselves to your company. Once you have accepted them as a client, you have agreed to respect your part of that commitment. Canceling your contract or reneging on a promise because of a better opportunity is an amateurish way to do business.

If you cancel an appointment, make sure it is for a good reason and not simply to transfer your attention to another client. Every time you have to cancel, make sure it is for a good reason. If the customer did not request the cancellation, have a valid explanation for why you need to cancel.

Everyone, at one time or another, will be tempted to improve their position at the risk of going back on their word. Do the right thing and uphold your commitment to your customers, no matter what the cost.

Don't give out personal information

Personal information is personal. When you begin to feel comfortable with a returning customer, it's easy to see the glass as half full and not half empty. Most people prefer to stay positive and not consider the way some people can complicate personal lives with unnecessary drama. Sadly, many workers have placed themselves in compromising and embarrassing situations simply by being nice and sharing personal information.

Be selective and careful when you give out personal information. Your last name, contact information, on-line social media screen names, and the coffee houses you frequent reveal the kind of information a customer can use to contact you away from work. Protect valuable information such as your marital status, children, and type of vehicle you drive.

Even when you want a relationship you have formed at work to be long-lasting, be extremely selective in how forthcoming you are with this personal information. There are too many people in this world with bad intentions.

Don't assume that everyone you come in contact with is harmless and has your best interests at heart. Don't give out personal information that might compromise you and the many things you have worked so hard to achieve.

Don't focus attention on good-looking customers

You are working with the public, so you can expect that some of the people you meet will be very attractive. They might be exceptionally well dressed or have amazing physiques or attractive facial features. Be very careful not to stare or ogle. It will be obvious to everyone.

Some people work very hard on their appearance. For others, their beauty is just natural. When you notice a customer who is pleasing to your eyes, be careful in the manner you approach and interact with them. While they might appreciate a compliment, they are not necessarily looking for one.

Your eye contact, body movements, gestures, and verbal interactions could be taken the wrong way if you deliver them in the wrong way. Treat everyone the same. No one should be treated more favorably just because they look better than another customer. All customers deserve equal treatment.

Preferential treatment can also work against you in the minds of the people who came in with your customer. These family members and friends will notice the special treatment. Obvious discriminatory behavior will reflect badly upon you and your company. Be discreet when you admire customers.

Don't steal from your employer

Sticky fingers is a character flaw that will stain your record and will follow you for years to come, severely hampering your ability to get a job in the future.

It usually begins with small, insignificant items that you wouldn't expect to be missed, such as office supplies or other items. But thievery is an addiction that leads to bigger theft that can end in termination and criminal prosecution.

A few employees rationalize theft as an entitlement or a substitute for low wages or missed promotions. These are merely excuses to justify criminal behavior. Don't be tempted to participate in this activity. It is wrong, unacceptable, and indefensible.

If you are tempted, consider the enormous risk you take when you go down this road. It won't matter how stellar an employee or representative you have been. Stealing from your employer will erase the positive reputation and exemplary employee status you worked so hard to create.

Don't stereotype people

Don't stereotype your customers. It is disrespectful to draw a conclusion about a customer based upon their looks, mannerisms, or other generalization. Profiling someone is always wrong, and most employers will never tolerate it. Sadly, too many customers have already suffered because of stereotyping. In some cases the stereotype or indifference may have been subtle. But even facial expressions and body movements can be viewed as disrespectful. A customer standing before you is just that: a customer who does not stand for any political party, ethnicity, religion, or country.

If you feel, for any reason, that your customer might be better served by someone else, then by all means enlist a co-worker. Personality clashes with customers are not uncommon. You cannot be expected to mesh with every personality you encounter. You should, however, avoid expressing any feelings of discontent, whether they are justified or not.

Don't criticize the clothes, behavior, or mannerisms of others. Give every customer the benefit of the doubt, and never jump to a conclusion about them before you actually know them.

Refrain from sexually explicitness

When you are talking to a customer, conduct yourself respectfully and appropriately. Avoid any dialog that could be questionable.

There are many sexually charged words that have made their way into the public mainstream. Nevertheless, don't assume these words or phrases are okay to use simply because you hear them "all the time" on television or in music. Strike these words from your vocabulary.

Sexually-driven dialog is a deal breaker for most customers. Using off-color dialog, even if it is popular, reflects poorly on you. You are in a position of greater respect and authority than the average person. Act like it! No customer is pleased when you reduce yourself to the level of street talk.

Exercise restraint when you speak to customers. Sexual innuendo is better left for your off-the-clock activities. Customers will respect you more when you choose your words carefully.

ALWAYS REMEMBER!

Customer service is everything!

You can improve your work ethic, establish a positive rapport, gain respect, and enhance your reputation simply by paying attention to the things that affect great customer service. Pay special attention to all things related to customer satisfaction. This will help your relationship with your employer and enhance your customer's experience.

The more serious you are about improving your performance, the more likely you are to reap the rewards and benefits of your job. When you commit yourself to perfecting your customer service model, you give your employer another reason to value you as an employee. You are also setting yourself up for long term success. Employers will respond faster to your improvements in customer service than to anything else you learn, train for, or prepare.

Many people believe that only special training in sales and marketing can improve financial success. They are only partially correct. A sales and marketing campaign is most likely to be successful when customer service is factored into the equation. You can have the best sales training in the world, but that will mean nothing if you don't have people skills!

Perfecting your mastery of customer service is one of the best kept secrets for achieving your long term goals. Approach customer service with commitment and passion. Once you master these skills, the sky is your limit!

two

Customer Service IS Sales!

One misconception about customer service is that it is not directly associated with sales. We have been conditioned to think of customer service as the warm-up act to the sales process. Nothing could be further from the truth! Customer service *is* sales!

The two are intertwined, and without one, the other would never function efficiently. Yet, we still observe educational materials that focus solely upon sales in an effort to achieve success and maximize profits. The concept of sales is marketed very heavily. Service, on the other hand, receives only minimal attention, and there is an assumption that it only needs to be adequate.

This cart-before-the-horse mindset is no different from thinking about the touchdown without considering the drive up the field. It's like dreaming of an Academy Award without ever starring in a motion picture. Products and services don't sell themselves! A sales pitch is useless unless it is built on a foundation of trust and respect with a customer. While the aroma in a coffee house might help to create the perfect mood for purchasing a cup of coffee, it is the employees and their level of service that seals the deal. In fact, without them there would be no aroma to begin with!

Happy customers with lots of money don't simply show up at your door and spend indiscriminately. The sale is the culmination of a successful journey that began with personal interaction, rapport, and peace of mind, qualities achieved during the customer service stage.

Like a marriage, a successful sales exchange needs to be complimented by great customer service for the transaction to be successful, and vice versa. This chapter focuses on companies and industries that have dedicated their efforts to achieving excellence in the field of customer service. It will help you better understand what customers expect of you. It will also detail how patience and timing can be utilized to your benefit.

A Model for Success

While you were a young child, many things in your upbringing influenced you and made you the person you are today. Perhaps it was a parent, school teacher, or coach who provided guidance and direction at a time when you needed it most. The lessons that shaped your upbringing were probably not identified or appreciated until much later on. Only when you look back do you begin to understand the profound impact these formative years had on your life.

As people get older, they tend to search out methods of self-improvement. They seek out business models and mentors who can offer valuable assistance for achieving goals. In customer service, the lessons don't always come naturally. People develop techniques from proven methods that are established and effective.

The examples contained here will provide a perfect footing to find successful, well-known customer service models. Once you understand these models, you will be able to develop similar techniques that you can immediately use. Study them and use them to your benefit.

The same lessons that influenced your upbringing can still shape your career in your adult years. The difference is that now you are using them to further your career, make more money, and become more successful. Look to established business models to draw your inspiration from. They can make all the difference to your career.

The Hotel Industry

There are no established, universal regulatory standards for customer service in the retail, service, and hospitality industries. There is, however, a common standard that has been adopted within the hotel industry. This standard or rating system has been adopted by other industries as well. The hotel industry rates properties and service by using a standard of one to five stars. A five-star Hotel represents accommodations and service that are unsurpassed. Regardless of the business you are in, you need to be well-regarded for your level of service as well as your products.

To deliver five-star service, you must first anticipate a customer's wants, needs, and expectations. Before they ever meet you in person or over the telephone, customers have an expectation of how the experience should go. Your ability to anticipate the service they expect will place you in a far better position to accommodate them. The best way to do this is with a proactive approach that anticipates their expectations.

When customers walk into a five-star hotel, they expect a lot more than when they walk into a three-star hotel. The service in the five-star establishment is expected to be superior. Although their expectations might be lower while they enjoy their time at a three-star hotel, you can be certain that they still expect consistency from the three-star service.

If you work in an industry that is not highly regarded, just imagine the great reputation you would have if you created service that caters to your customers with the same excellence as the finest hotel or upscale restaurant does. When you deliver service above and beyond your customers' expectations, you make customers for life. Develop and deliver Five-Star customer service, no matter what your customer might be expecting.

Customers care about being taken care of. When you treat them well, they feel more comfortable doing business with you. Consumer confidence is one of the leading economic indicators that measure sales on a national level. You can now begin to understand how customer service ties in directly to sales. Five-star service equals satisfied customers. Satisfied customers feel more confident to do business with you. Consumer confidence also equals a robust economy. It's a win-win situation that benefits everyone... and it all starts with customer service!

Recognize the importance of five-star service when you develop your customer service model. Always work to deliver service above what your customer expects. Don't just meet customer expectations; take them to the stars!

The Wedding Industry

One of the fascinating aspects of the wedding industry is that dozens of people from several different businesses must work together for months just to achieve the objective of two customers. It's even more amazing that many of these workers will never actually meet, yet they will rely on each other's efforts to achieve the customer's satisfaction.

Banquet facilities open their doors to many on-site wedding vendors so that they can provide service effectively. For example, the wedding cake might be supplied by an outside company, but the facility will supply the cake table. The facility staff also slices and serves the wedding cake to the guests.

This cooperative effort extends further out. Consider the minister, for example. Most ministers supply their talents to officiate the ceremony while they rely on a disc jockey or the venue itself to supply the microphone and amplifier. Most ministers don't possess these tools of the trade, yet they need them to complete their part of the wedding services.

These are only two of the many examples where teamwork achieves a common purpose for a single customer. Even though these vendors have never met each other, an unwritten but universal code of cooperation works to get the job done. If you work cooperatively with others on behalf of your customer, you will be praised for your success in marrying the customer service efforts of many people.

The Airline Industry

If you have ever flown on Southwest Airlines, you have enjoyed customer service that has placed it among the most endeared companies in the nation. One of the best examples of their customer service is the manner in which their flight attendants describe the safety features and evacuation procedures before take-off. Over the years, fliers have enjoyed some very comical, yet informative, explanations of their pre-flight safety procedures. It is not uncommon to hear celebrity impersonations, rhythmic rap dialog, or comedic one-liners.

This is a deliberate form of customer service. It alleviates several fears that many people have about flying. Some people feel tense and stressed when they board an airplane. There are a number of reasons for this stress: confinement in tight quarters, unusual air circulation, sitting next to strangers, or medical conditions such as vertigo. Whatever the reason for their discomfort, the Southwest routine replaces the tension with ease and relaxation that contributes to the travel experience. It also fosters a personable and approachable reputation for the flight attendants.

Great customer service does not have to consist of things that you can see on the surface. If you look deeper into the fears that trouble some of your customers, you can alleviate those issues and provide a degree of comfort from the outset. If you are involved in an industry that has a less-than-favorable reputation, find ways to address this issue head on. Let your customer know that you are aware of their concern and that you have a remedy that will set their mind at ease. Just like a flight attendant, you provide comfort to your customers by focusing on an issue that addresses their fears.

The Insurance Industry

Customer service is enacted each and every day on television. You see examples of helpful workers assisting employees with products and services throughout the commercials and other programming. You also see deliberate attempts to promise customer service long before a relationship is established.

For years, the insurance industry has promoted "peace of mind" as the most important element for a customer to consider. This on-going industry-wide advertising campaign brilliantly uses customer service as the main incentive to purchase their products.

Their slogans say it all: "Like a good neighbor, State Farm is there" . . . "You're in good hands with All State" . . . "So easy a caveman can do it" . . . "Nationwide is on your side." They are implying that they are there to assist you in a worry-free manner. While insurance companies clearly have a product to sell, they realize that a just-the-facts-ma'am description of insurance products is probably not all that exciting to customers. Here again, the sales appeal is customer service!

Insurance company marketing campaigns exhibit one of the finest customer service models in business today. Their very public portrayal of how they take care of their customers has been a feature of the industry for several decades. Look at established advertising campaigns to get useful ideas for your own customer service model. When you follow the "customer comes first" example of the insurance companies, you will establish an unbeatable model for success!

The Cruise Ship Industry

The cruise ship industry illustrates another example of a sales appeal focused around customer service. The cruise experience is all about taking care of a customer's every need. It promises a red carpet feeling in which every person is treated above and beyond their expectations. The interesting thing about the cruise industry is that it is so multi-faceted. It begins with the sales process and continues on-board with the finest accommodations, food service, entertainment, recreation, and shore tours, to name a few.

Regardless of the amenities provided, the service is still the same. The customer is king, and the experience and service is designed to be exemplary and consistent. This consistency is reflective of a "can do" attitude in which employees from different sectors step in to help customers, no matter if it is part of their job description or not.

These floating cities offer a first glimpse into what it would be like if a city on dry land were to adopt a customer service ordinance. Think about it! If each worker in a city was committed to making each customer's experience incredible, it would probably be the most productive city in the world. Perhaps city officials should look seriously at the cruise industry for inspiration and guidance. You can learn much by looking at diverse business models. If you can appropriately offer a consistent level of customer service while delivering the many unique elements of your business, you can provide an experience your customer can enjoy in many different ways. Explore ways to enhance customer experiences through offering multi-faced customer service.

The Magic of Disney

Millions of satisfied customers have enjoyed the exemplary customer service provided by the Disney Corporation. For companies and consumers alike, Disney has become the quintessential model of customer service that exceeds nearly every level of expectation. Their exceptional customer satisfaction can be experienced in every one of their consumer-oriented properties—theme parks, hotels, motion pictures, concerts, retail stores, etc. Disney's customer service policies and practices continue to set the standard by which nearly every business in professional commerce is measured.

Visitors to a Disney Theme Park enjoy a pleasant experience made possible by a crew of helpful employees, who are given the moniker of "cast members." Each cast member receives training in the ethical standards and responsibilities of dealing with the public. The Disney Corporation realizes that the environment and atmosphere at their theme parks is created by helpful cast members, who maximize the experience of their guests. Do you see the connection yet? Guests might visit the park for the rides and amenities, but their experience is maximized by their cast members. Similarly, customers might show up for your products and services, but their experience will be maximized by your ability to be helpful and accommodating!

One of the phenomenal aspects of Disney's customer service is a little known practice known as "Making a Magical Moment." Several times during the day, supervisors will encourage cast members to go out and "make a magical moment." This entails giving them flexibility and freedom to do something special for a park guest.

From randomly handing out Fast Passes, to surprising a little girl to be a Fairy Godmother in Training, to inviting an entire family to help Mickey open the park for the day, the stories of Magical Moments created by cast members are as legendary as the Disney name itself.

You may have witnessed parades at Disney Theme Parks and wondered how some visitors become Grand Marshals and others get the opportunity to ride on floats in the parade. Well, now you know! It wasn't because they knew someone or paid a fee. Many people are chosen daily to become honorary citizens of the park and share in a Magical Moment of their own. All this is made possible by the Disney family of cast members who take customer service to a memorable level.

These examples should motivate you to explore unique ways to satisfy your customers and guests. If you can create a remarkable moment by simple acts of kindness or unexpected forms of appreciation, the impact this can have upon your reputation is unlimited. Every interaction with your customers is an opportunity for you to create a memorable moment.

Almost every parent has taken their children to the doctor for an exam or shots. For years, doctors, nurses, and assistants have been known to offer a colorful sticker, balloon, toy, or lollipop to kids after the appointment. This random act of kindness is a form of customer service, but it's hardly random. It pleases the parent just as much as the child. It relaxes the kids, softens the emotional impact of the experience, encourages a "thank you" (good manners), and generally makes life easier for parents. There are many ways we can create memorable moments by offering simple but effective forms of customer service.

Recap of Industry Models

The examples above: Five-Star service, codes of cooperation, easing customer fears, promoting peace of mind, providing multi-faceted offerings, and creating magical moments—are all established methods that can be applied to your customer service blueprint. Each time you adopt one of these proven principles, you inch yourself closer to delivering satisfying experiences to your customers, co-workers, and employer.

Whatever your employment may be, the lessons here will be just as impactful as the mentorship you received in your younger years; they will be with you for a lifetime. They will advance you through this and future positions. They will enable you to achieve more income, respect, and promotions throughout your career.

Continue to be inspired by successful companies, popular industries, and national advertising campaigns. If someone is advertising it or putting it into practice, chances are it's working for them! You don't have to spend thousands of dollars for personal consulting fees in order to establish great customer service. Look to established companies and industries for proven ways to create a model for success!

Develop Your "B" Sides

Thus far you have received some practical tips that you can implement immediately to enhance your interactions with customers. However if you are constantly looking for that edge that will set you apart from everyone else in your field, the following concept may give you just the edge you need to develop a customer service model that is unique and specialized.

It begins in the music industry and the deliberate marketing campaign it used for decades to attract customers. To understand why it is useful, you have to look deep into the framework of the recording industry. It is a never-before-explored element that can change your entire perspective on the way to do business. It offers a proven methodology that will inspire and motivate change in your life and your business. It will enhance your work ethic and improve your customer service model. And it was all made possible by a seven-inch-round vinyl record.

First A Little History

Long before the age of personal computers, downloadable music, and hand-held playback devices, there were vinyl records. The most popular type was the 45 rpm platter. Vinyl records were enjoyed by consumers, played in jukeboxes, and broadcast by disc jockeys worldwide. They were the quintessential method of playing recorded music from the 1950's to the 1980's.

The design of the vinyl record was very simple. It included an "A" side and a "B" side. The A side would contain the primary hit; this is the song that the record companies would promote. The B side would normally include a relatively unknown song by the same artist. While the A side single was heavily promoted, the B side received very little attention. Its purpose was to give the listener a glimpse into the consistency of the artist's talents. By showcasing this versatility, record companies hoped the record-buyer would find another reason to like the artist. In essence, B side songs were there to compliment the A side hit.

The Food Chain

Record companies had a very deliberate plan for each 45 rpm record. Radio disc jockeys would play the A side of the record. The plan assumed that the listener would enjoy the song enough to go out and purchase the "single" from their local record store. The record company assumed the consumer would also listen to the B side of the record. The hope was that consumers would enjoy the versatility and consistency of the artist enough to consider buying full-length, 12-inch, 33rpm record albums by the artist. Once the consumer purchased this 33 rpm record, the snowball process of building a fan had begun. The record company assumed that, once a consumer bought an album, the consumer would now support the artist with additional purchases of concert tickets, more vinyl records, merchandise, etc.

Once the customer became a fan of an artist, the record company assumed the consumer would support the artist by watching a scheduled appearance on television. When this happened, commercial advertisers also benefited. Commercial relationships like these are vital to television stations and their programming. Thus, while it was not the hit, the B side single served a very important role in the food chain of the record industry.

A Record Change

These vinyl records were about to serve another unexpected use. Radio disc jockeys who played the A side would occasionally flip the records over and cue-up the B side to preview it off-the-air. Occasionally, they would discover hidden gems on the other side of these platters. Sometimes, these songs were played on the air and became new hit singles in their own right. Songs that were originally written off by the record company now became hit records. This happened time and time again. "Unchained Melody" by the Righteous Brothers, "Maggie May" by Rod Stewart, "La Bamba" by Richie Valens and "I Will Survive" by Gloria Gaynor were all recorded on the B side. They rose to popularity because they were given a chance by a radio DJ who felt their potential was worth showcasing.

These are just a few of the songs that were never meant to be hits yet became the defining songs in the catalog of the artist. The success of these and other songs occurred because someone saw their potential and took a chance.

No less effort went into producing the B side single than went into the A side single. From beginning to end, the songwriters and musicians had great belief in the song's success. They spent hundreds of hours writing, rehearsing, and recording each song. Their investment of time and effort was substantial. Only upon completion of the track did the record company deem its commercial appeal to be substandard. Nevertheless, the B side songs proved to be a useful contribution to the record industry.

Applying This Concept to Customer Service

Think about the talents you have that you are not using to their full potential. These are your B sides. They may have been relegated to the lower end of your list of skills. Focus on them and bring them up to par. Develop them and nurture them. Bring them into your customer service model and give them a chance to succeed.

Take a thorough accounting of your unique personality traits, hobbies, and characteristics that you can incorporate into your customer service model. They might be your passions or simply traits for which you have been complimented. Come up with a plan for developing and using these skills productively at work.

What are the skills you practice at home with your kids, with computers, navigating social media websites, or programming your telephone? Maybe you have an engaging personality, a sense of humor, or an ability to tell stories. Perhaps it's your linguistic talents, writing skills, or your ability to decipher detailed instructions. Whatever the case, you have many untapped skills that are there to be discovered and used. In these secondary skills, you are going to find diversity, stand-alone techniques, and new service strengths.

It may take years for a tree to bear fruit. The same is true for the evolution of a discovery or development, such as that of B sides. The record industry ran with this model for more than forty years. Why? Because it worked! In nearly every case, the alternate selection became used and enjoyed. Give the B sides in your life and business the opportunity to succeed. Just like the radio DJs of yesterday, you have the ability to showcase some great sides of you that are just waiting to be enjoyed by others!

Meeting Customer Expectations

"Isn't it better to exceed expectations, instead of just meeting them?" Without a doubt! However, before you can exceed expectations, you must know what it means to meet them! What do customers expect of you? What are they focusing on? What concerns them most? When you can answer these questions, then you can begin to establish a level of service that exceeds them.

Besides all the things you choose to include in your A to Z model, customers have A to Z lists of their own. These include the characteristics that customers evaluate with every interaction. Once you recognize these, you are one step closer to a satisfied customer.

Whether you are aware of it or not, customers size up your every word and gesture. Every mannerism and nuance of your demeanor is constantly being scrutinized. Most customers don't even know they are doing this. While some might study your degree of customer service intently, others simply rely on their natural instinct and their comfort zone.

You use your natural instincts, too. Whenever you ride a bike, comb your hair, or put on your shoes, you are depending on your instinctive nature. Certain things come naturally, and if they feel right, people don't think much about them. But if they feel wrong, then warning flags go up all over the place. When people are uncomfortable around someone, their first and natural reaction is one of avoidance and apprehensiveness. Most people distance themselves from people and situations that don't feel right.

Customers evaluate you according to a number of criteria, including the following attributes. By understanding these, you will better understand what customers expect of you and what fits naturally in their comfort zone. Study these attributes and use them to develop a standard that showcases your efforts in the best light possible.

Attitude A customer can tell if you are having a bad day or not. It's all in the manner in which you express yourself. Your mood is vital for customers to be drawn to you. Always project a positive attitude that invites them into the conversation. Smile and be genuinely interested in assisting them!

Behavior "Actions speak louder than words!" Behavior is defined as a manner of acting. The way you act in the presence of your customers is important. Think of your behavior like a silent film from the 1930's: it speaks volumes through your actions!

Character This is a moral and ethical quality. Moral character is demonstrated; it cannot be demonstrated verbally. Either you have it or you don't. By being mindful of the things you do and the way you do them, you can demonstrate a pleasant and genuine character to everyone you meet.

Dedication People can tell in a very short period of time if you are passionate about your job or simply going through the motions. Your verbal interactions and body language should exude a confidence and willingness to get the job done. When a customer perceives this, they know they are doing business with the right person!

Etiquette This is the collection of rules for presenting yourself. It is rooted in traditional values. Socially it is known as an established manner of ethical behavior. Show a level of decorum and etiquette that is upscale and proper, not juvenile. Customers expect class when you serve them, no matter if it is in a retail, service, or hospitality environment.

Flexibility This is your ability to take care of your customer on many different levels and your ability to please them by changing or conforming. You don't live in a one-size-fits-all world. The diversity of your products and services is as wide ranging as the customers you serve. You can complement this diversity by being open and flexible to the new ideas that promise unique ways to satisfy your customer.

Good Posture Did you know that folding your arms in front of you gives the impression that you are standoffish and not approachable? This and other examples of bad posture can give your customer a negative impression of you. Sit, stand, and gesture in a manner that sends a message of confidence. This allows your customer to feel at ease when they do business with you.

Honesty To understand the true meaning of honesty, you need to look at its opposite meanings: deceit and fraud. Customers are intuitive. They can spot dishonesty a mile away. Be fair, truthful, and sincere in everything you do.

Integrity Your Integrity is your adherence to moral and ethical principles—the soundness of your moral character. Integrity is the foundation of your reputation. Without integrity, the bottom falls out of your structure. Maintain standards that are rich in principles and ethics. Your customers will notice and appreciate you for it.

Judgment "It's your call." Many things in our responsibility are judgment calls. Customers often look to you for direction, because you are considered the expert. They also expect you to make reasonable judgments that can make their experience more pleasant. Learn how much authority you have to make judgment calls. You don't necessarily have to stretch the rules, but you can stretch your willingness to do more for your customer.

Knowledge Customers expect you to know what you are talking about. By the very fact that someone hired you to do a specific job, your customers assume you are well-trained and knowledgeable. Go above and beyond the traditional training you receive by learning as much as you can about the products and services you represent.

Loyalty Everyone wants loyal customers. Customers, too, want and expect you to be loyal to them and to the business you represent. There is nothing wrong about expressing satisfaction with your employer and your profession, and there's a lot right about it. Your loyalty is their reassurance!

Manners These are the foundation of professional behavior. Good manners are universal in every culture and in every country around the globe. Your manners are one of the elements a customer will fondly remember about you long after the sale is completed. Some things never go out of style; good manners are one of them!

Personality Customers seek a pleasant experience when they shop for goods and services. Your personality is an important part of their happy experience. Too much personality may be overwhelming. Too little might prove uninteresting. Find a neutral balance that lets the strengths of your personality shine through.

Sound Business Practices Customers also expect you to practice sound business principles. Anything less than professional business practices and ethics is unacceptable. Study your business practices, refine them, and show them to all of your customers.

Temperament Are you cool under pressure? The way you react to situations in the work place also influences customer satisfaction. A customer can sense your tension and stress. They may choose to distance themselves from you or the business if you are too "hyper." When you are faced with difficult circumstances, stay calm and composed.

Understanding A fundamental part of your employee-customer exchanges is based upon real human emotion. These exchanges are influenced by your ability to empathize with your customers' concerns. This is especially important during exchanges and returns. Your ability to be understanding is a very powerful force. It is important and always appreciated by customers.

Vocabulary Your verbal communication skills are important to your customers. They will listen intently to what you have to say. Pay close attention to your vocabulary, and search for ways to establish a verbal exchange that encourages their participation.

Any one of these factors can make or break a sale. So much more than the sales pitch goes into sales. Customers may never express to you that these are important. But you can bet they are!

A customer will never walk up to you and say, "tell me about your integrity?", or "how is your temperament?" or "your good posture turns me off." Expecting that kind of directness is unrealistic. This is why it is so important to look deeper into the things that customers are concerned about.

Put yourself in the shoes of the customer. Have you ever been repulsed when a sales person has lacked any of these characteristics? If not, you're a rare person indeed.

Always keep in mind that you are the face of the company you represent. There might be a spokesperson who promotes the products, or services your company sells. But the moment you are face-to-face with a customer, you and only you are the face of the company. How you respond to your customer's expectations will determine the success of each transaction.

Wait for it ... Wait for it ... Swing!

"Good things come to those who wait!"

When you show patience in making decisions, you make better, more informed decisions. In customer service, your ability to search out the right opportunity can make all the difference in the world.

In sports competition, it's all about timing. On the gridiron, seasoned quarterbacks know the advantages of being patient in the pocket. This allows them to study the weaknesses in their opponent's defense and connect at just the right moment. Marathon runners and bicyclists periodically conserve their energy and then surge at different intervals so as to time their success. In baseball, batting coaches train players to observe each pitch intently and patiently await the perfect opportunity to swing.

Customer satisfaction is built on the same principle. The goal is to connect with your customers effectively at precisely the right moment. This book, Customer Service A to Z, has been written to redefine the traditional mindset. It is simply not enough to show up, smile, and win over a customer. You need to earn their trust, respect, and confidence. You can accomplish this through the use of proven techniques and precise timing.

Patience and timing in our society are underrated. They are time-honored traditions, just as practical in stock trading on Wall Street as they are in planning a vacation. They are important parts of winning wars and negotiating treaties. We have seen how the timing of emergency responders has saved lives and how the patience of waiting out a storm has prevented catastrophes. Even history reminds us that "Rome wasn't built in a day!"

Patience and timing are just as important in customer interactions. There is a time to approach, a time to assist, and a time to step back. There is a time to be informative and a time to let the customer speak. The ability to sense these moments is instrumental for delivering great customer service.

A baseball player doesn't just step up the plate and hit the ball. It might look that easy, but hitting a baseball is one of the hardest things to do in all of sports. Many different pitches may come his way. So much depends on other factors, as well. For example; the pitcher, the score, the following batter, the count (balls and strikes), the batter's record (runs, hits, ability to steal bases, etc.), the batter's stance (right or left handed) are all important factors for the batter and coach to think about before the pitch is ever thrown.

In baseball, they call it the strike zone. The pitcher tries to get the batter to "swing and miss" at pitches that are thrown in or near the strike zone. Batting coaches have conditioned their players to "wait for it…wait for it…swing!" They encourage players to wait for that perfect opportunity to connect with the ball. It's a strategy that has many similarities to the sales process.

Customers are searching for the perfect products and services. They are looking for a fair price, helpful people to assist them, and a reputable company to do business with. Businesses are looking to attract these customers and connect with them in the hopes of making satisfied returning customers. Each wants to achieve their objective. The only difference is that baseball is a competition.

Since there is no competition between you and your customer, the only challenge is to make each party feel comfortable with each other.

In baseball, each pitch that comes over the plate represents an opportunity for the batter to "hit it out of the park." In business, each encounter represents another opportunity to have a satisfied customer.

When a customer is before you, practice the "wait for it" philosophy. Seek the perfect opportunity to offer the first greeting and assistance. Follow-up when it is appropriate, and try to pick up the signs a customer might be giving you. Sometimes customers need some alone time to think. At other times, they might need more information. Customers don't like to be crowded, and sometimes they don't know what questions to ask. Know when to lead, know when to follow, and know when to get out of the way! If you practice this approach with each customer, you will develop a natural rhythm that feels comfortable for both of you.

Customer Service IS Sales
Chapter Recap

This chapter has looked at successful customer service models in other industries and discussed how these approaches have increased sales (A Model for Success). It has examined cutting-edge techniques used for decades by the record industry that can still be used to develop a different side of you (Develop your B sides). It has established the core element of customer expectations in order for you to apply a more efficient customer service model (Meeting Customer Expectations). Finally, it has addressed how perfect timing can be used in a sales transaction (Wait for it...Wait for it...Swing!).

These techniques are vital to each sales transaction. They provide definitive proof that customer service is instrumental in sales. No longer can it be said that customer service is the window dressing to a sales transaction. Service is more important than any other single factor of a successful transaction. Every business wants sales, and customer service makes sales possible.

That's why Customer Service IS Sales!!!

Three

Changing Public Perception

A perception is defined as the act of understanding, or comprehending something through the use of intuition. In part, perception can be achieved through the senses, the mind, or other faculty. It can be as simple as insight or recognition. Perceptions allow people to formulate opinions based on what they know or feel to be true. Because perceptions can be based on popular knowledge, perceptions are not always based in fact.

This chapter stresses the importance of recognizing the popular perceptions that customers have. Understanding their way of thinking is important. So too is the way you respond to them. You have unique characteristics and implement sales techniques and standards that are different from your customers. Once you have identified your customers' perceptions, you can develop techniques that respond more sensitively to their needs and, at times, redirect their way of thinking.

Make a Great First Phone Impression

Your telephone approach says a lot more than just the words you're speaking.

In business, many first impressions are made over the telephone. From the very first words spoken to the automated operator, your customer begins developing opinions of you and the business you represent. Each telephone call is like the fresh canvas in front of an artist beginning a new painting. It's a clean slate. Just like an artist, you establish the direction and destine a successful or failed outcome early on.

First, a Few Words

Sometimes the little things you say or do not say make a difference. For example, how do you answer the telephone at work? Do you say, "Hi," "Hello," or "What's up?" Or do you answer the phone with a pleasant and inviting greeting? That is the first thing a customer expects. When you answer your telephone with your company name, you invite the impression that you exercise the professionalism they hoped you had in the first place. In addition, phrases like "how may I help you?" offer immediate comfort and direction to the person on the other end of the line.

An Acute Sense of Perception

A customer has more acute perception when talking to you on the telephone in much the same way as people without sight do. In a conversation, a customer can hear you smile, gauge your interest or non-interest, and sense your apprehensiveness. Smile when you use the telephone; it helps you begin your conversation on a sound footing. A smile changes the intonation of your voice and has an immediately effect on your customers.

When customers call a department store or a grocery store, they expect the person on the other end of the line to be accommodating, helpful, and eager to assist them. They want to receive information from a knowledgeable representative who welcomes making their acquaintance, not someone who simply approaches the conversation in a lackadaisical fashion.

Thank You... Thank You Very Much!

You can learn a lot from The King of Rock & Roll, Elvis Presley. In his concerts and other live appearances, he used many sayings, such as "Thank you, thank you very much," "You're a fantastic audience," and "You're beautiful!" This was his very deliberate way of endearing himself to his audience. We can all learn from his lesson.

There is no better way to improve the way a customer sees you than to ingratiate yourself. This opens new doors and forestalls potential conflicts. When Elvis delivered one of his signature lines, he did it as a sincere demonstration of the appreciation he truly felt for his fans. If you extend a sincere and believable willingness to assist your customers, you can make all the difference in the world. This is a simple but effective example to learn from. Sincerity can do wonders for your reputation. They didn't call him The King for nothing.

Exercise this same sincerity by supporting your customer's decision to do business with you. If they are interested in a product or service you provide, acknowledge their efforts to contact you. Offer them the options that complement the product or service they are considering. When you acknowledge the decisions clients have made, you reinforce their choice to travel down this road with you. And is there a better way to discuss your products and services than affirming that they have made a great decision in their efforts to gather more information?

First Point of Contact

Many negative perceptions that customers carry around with them today are the result of bad experiences over the telephone. What you say on the telephone is every bit as important as what you say on the sales floor. The fact you are not meeting face-to-face does not mean you can be casual about the customer service you provide.

You can impact with every customer by cultivating positive rapport over the telephone. This first point of contact is the first glimpse a customer will get of your personality, speaking ability, and professionalism. The sincere and appreciative manner in which you approach telephone sales and service will change public perception for the better.

Consider the Visual Impression You Make

Every time you dress, your image lingers.

Each time you are in front of customers, they form perceptions of you. They notice the clothing you wear and the way you wear it. You are under scrutiny. No matter the business you represent, your visual appearance needs to reflect well in the eyes of your customers. For this discussion, let's focus upon the retail sales floor at a typical shopping mall.

In many businesses, especially larger chain stores and franchises, you will find great uniformity of dress among the sales associates. This uniformity is often required by company mandated attire and standards, because employers with dress codes can expect few problems with dress code violations among their employees. When problems do crop up, they are often associated with clothing that is baggy, not tucked in or wrinkled.

Many privately owned businesses permit a more tolerant approach to sales floor attire. Sometimes dress is left entirely to the employee's discretion. The practice assumes that a casual style will be more aligned with the customers, allowing them to feel more comfortable. Another common practice is to require employees to wear a particular color and style of pant, shirt, or skirt. This often leads to a loosely based dress code that is meant to produce a casual uniformity.

Making a Fashion Statement

No matter what type of attire employees are required to wear, what's important is how their appearance will be perceived by the customer. After all, it is the customer's opinion that matters most! Casual attire may be perceived by some customers as everyday street clothing that conveys the message to customers that the employees or the company gives little thought or preparation to the visual impression they make. When clothing looks tattered or unkempt, customers can feel the urge to distance themselves from that particular sales associate, and perhaps even from the store.

Customers have expectations. They expect a sales associate in an auto parts store to be dressed significantly different than one in a fine jewelry store. The store environment and the products sold also create expectations about the way employees should present themselves. To be effective in winning a customer's trust, respect, and business, employees must meet or exceed the expectations of their clientele.

There is no universal protocol or established standard for workplace fashion. But think of dress as a key factor in customer relations. Whenever you dress appropriately on the job, you add a certain amount of class to a customer's shopping experience. Customers feel comfortable doing business with you if you present yourself as a respectable businessperson. You broadcast to every onlooker the true character of the establishment you represent. And this begins with your attire. Even if the setting is not formal, you still wield a tremendous tool for influencing perception if you simply pay attention to the way you dress.

The Winner by Unanimous Decision

An unlikely example of this is a boxing match. There is really nothing glamorous or elegant about an event like this. In the ring two half-naked men try their best to knock the daylights out of each other. It's what they've trained for. Between rounds, the fighters spit into a bucket while their trainer gives them instructions on how best to punish their opponent. The ring crew treats them with the efficiency of a race car pit crew, tending their wounds and to stop all bleeding and swelling that go along with the job. While this is going on, a bikini-clad girl walks around the ring every three minutes, holding a ring card and teasing the men in the audience with a few brief seconds of scripted eye candy. Meanwhile, the blood-thirsty audience cheers and jeers the fighter of their choice.

One element elevates the level of sophistication in the ring and transforms this otherwise blood-fest between gladiators into an upscale, sophisticated social event that appeals to every class of viewer. This is the formal presentation of the ring announcer. He is usually dressed in a tuxedo, moves with poise, and speaks with eloquence and near-perfect diction. His attire and demeanor stand alone and invite the audience to per-ceive the match as something dramatically different from what otherwise goes on in the ring.

The announcer elevates this from a spectacle to an elegant event suitable for celebrities and luminaries. You can do the same thing. Your business is certainly not a spectacle! But by dressing well and exhibiting an approachable demeanor and helpful attitude, you can make as much difference as the ring announcer. If a boxing match can be made respectable this easily, imagine what you can do with a business that is already respectable! In the process, you will enjoy greater business success and add a touch of elegance to your customers' shopping experience.

Are You As Funny As You Think You Are?

Wield the power of humor wisely.

Every time you speak with a customer, you need to conduct yourself in an appropriate manner. This is an unwritten code of conduct in every business. Every verbal interaction is extremely important. Don't run the risk of damaging your reputation by exercising poor judgment when you speak with customers. How you speak is just as important as how you deliver your words.

Catching the Signals

Customers are usually quite forgiving of honest mistakes, mispronunciations, and other slight defects in our normal speech. Humor, on the other hand, is a very deliberate action that is often scrutinized by your customers. When is humor acceptable? When should it be used cautiously? And when is humor better left unsaid? A traffic light analogy provides a helpful and responsible way to look at how we use humor.

Red Light—STOP: Humor Should Not Be Used!

Humor in the form of sexual innuendo, otherwise known as "blue" humor, can damage your reputation and that of the business you represent. So can edgy commentary on social issues and political humor. It's also a bad idea to direct humor unexpectedly at someone else, good

natured or otherwise, even someone you know. Humor is almost never appropriate in business situations unless you have already established a rapport with the customer.

Yellow Light—Approach Humor with CAUTION

If you have not discussed humor with your employer or supervisor, proceed with caution. For example, affluent customers of upscale businesses may have conservative values less tolerant of humor. Even customers of more casual businesses may still expect a G-rated environment. Humor can have an effect on future sales and referrals. Weigh the risks before you offer an unsolicited comment. If humor has not been discussed with your employer or supervisor, leave the humorous comment unsaid or at the very least, use it cautiously.

Green Light—GO: Humor Is Acceptable

You will certainly develop good relationships—even friendships—with some customers. Once you are confident that they know you and your sense of humor, you can judiciously introduce humor into your conversations. Perhaps you or your company has built a reputation as "interactive" or "vocally engaging." If that's the case, customers know what to expect. Be sure to discuss with your employer or supervisor whether the green light to humor is lit.

Speaking In Body Language

When a customer says or does something that invites a joke, an appropriate follow up through your timing and mannerisms instead of your words may be far more productive. For instance a simple tilt of your head, a dramatic pause, or a slow vocal reply may be the perfect response that does not cross any boundaries. You don't always have to communicate your humor with words. Sometimes, a gesture can communicate the same idea much more palatably than words.

Never take for granted the ability you have to influence matters simply by expressing yourself. You'll find out the hard way if you do not exercise good judgment and etiquette and introduce inappropriate humor. By contrast, using humor at just the right time can break the ice, make customers comfortable, and even close the sale!

An Unwritten Code of Conduct

Your image can attract customers.

How do people view your profession? Do they hold you and it in high esteem? Many people who work with the public are occasionally viewed with disdain because their profession is not glamorous or high in status. Negative stereotypes can result when others in the profession misbehave or offer poor service. Think of it as democracy. If the work force of an entire industry adhered to the same code-of-ethics, customers everywhere would have a favorable impression of both the workers and the industry!

Consider a profession that people love but know little about: the circus clown. The popular image of a clown suffers because of uninformed opinions about the nature of

the job. The very meaning of "clowning around" implies that the public does not need to take the clown seriously. It has been a persistent theme for years.

However, suppose you were engaged in a conversation with a stranger and told them you were a professional circus clown. What would you suppose their reaction would be? More often than not, you'll be met with a big smile, wide eyes, and an engaging conversation with a person who was fascinated by what you do. Most people like clowns and welcome the opportunity to learn more about a line of work they know little about.

So how is it that clowns are perceived so favorably and other vocations are not? The answer lies in the make-up of their profession (pun intended).

An Industry Standard

The unwritten code of conduct of the clown profession has set an industry standard for years. Besides the make-up and costumes, something else sets clowns apart from just about everyone else in the entertainment industry. All of these performers adhere to an "unwritten code of conduct" while they are in character. They maintain this stringent standard while they are performing. This helps to ensure the integrity of their character.

You will never see a clown use a public restroom, get dressed or undressed into their costume, smoke a cigarette, drink anything, use obscene gestures, chew gum, eat food, blow their nose, or talk on a cell phone. Often, they won't even speak unless it is part of their character. And they almost never touch guests beyond a handshake or a hand-on-a-shoulder for a photograph.

This unwritten code of conduct preserves the beloved character of the profession. Intentionally or unintentionally, clowns practice image awareness. To see a clown putting on his or her makeup, would take away from the image that the entire profession wants to cultivate. Nobody wants to see Bozo coming out of a bathroom stall or smoking a cigarette behind a rollercoaster.

These incredibly accomplished and dedicated performers work to maintain and preserve a distinct image. Everyone who enters the profession understands the importance of commitment and dedication, for maintaining the clown persona. It's their version of customer service. They have disciplined themselves for years to defend the integrity of their character in a fashion that leaves no room for error.

Develop Your Character

The time has come for the retail, service, and hospitality industries to raise the standards of professionalism. By defining control of what the customer experience should be, the industry can take charge of the image it portrays. You can do the same for your business. If you wish to be taken as seriously as a stage performer or be respected as much as a clown, you can learn from watching what performers do to maintain their image and reputation.

You have the talent, the ability, the educational standards, and the professionalism to make this happen. All you need to develop now is the discipline. Define your character and refine your image. You are a consummate professional who is aware of his or her surroundings. Now show it. And remain in character until the stage lights (the eyes of the public) are no longer on you.

When you develop your character and define your image with this sort of clarity, you will establish your own unwritten code of conduct that encourages your customers to hold you in high esteem.

The Honor System

Yes, you can borrow that . . . just be sure to bring it back.

By nature, most people trust one another. In nearly every society and every culture, regardless of the political or religious climate, people put faith in trust and honesty. Giving someone the benefit of the doubt is a time-honored tradition.

An Established History

Many times every day, you have opportunities to do the right thing and to reciprocate when someone else does it. Take restaurants for example. For as long as anyone can remember, the act of dining in a restaurant is predicated on trust that the customer will dine first and pay later. It is always possible that a customer will "dine and dash," but the time-honored practice is still to trust that the customer will follow the appropriate and unwritten protocol.

For many years, religious denominations and houses of worship placed tithing canisters in plain view of congregations without fear of being victimized. Some churches also had rows of candles aligned in prayer areas, where parishioners could light a candle and place a donation in the box provided. Honesty is expected, and the expectation is not often violated.

In many offices and other work environments, "snack boxes" can be seen in common areas. They are often put

there by outside vendors, who leave boxes full of candy, crackers, chips, and chocolate bars where employees of the company can enjoy them. Employees who take a snack are expected to abide by the honor system and leave the appropriate amount in the snack box.

The same sort of honor system is used with newspaper racks. The receptacles are designed to open when the proper coin amount is inserted. Nothing stops someone from walking away with ten copies of the daily newspaper. However, that seldom occurs. The unwritten rule of honesty allows the exercise of good intentions.

Or consider the carpool lane. Drivers are expected to follow the law and not take advantage of the carpool lane just because no squad cars are around. This system of trust benefits motorists and encourages everyone to make the daily commute function as smoothly as the congestion allows. For the most part, it works quite well. When it doesn't, other drivers resent the violator.

Being an Honorable Employee

Every profession can illustrate examples of trust and honesty being taken for granted. The honor system is an unwritten expectation that people will do the right thing. You'll see this faith all around you—in business, in community involvement, and in customer service.

Your store manager expects you to use good judgment when you are stocking merchandise after a shipment comes in. You would be irresponsible if you recklessly tossed or dropped products or allowed carts to damage store equipment, would you not? The manager trusts you to use common sense and show decency and good professional judgment.

Think about how the honor system applies to handicap parking spaces. No one appreciates it when someone parks in a place everyone knows is set aside for people who need it. The same can be said for cutting other drivers off or otherwise engaging in hazardous habits while driving a company vehicle.

The honor system is based on the expectation that people will *keep their word* when they interact with others. Handicapped spaces, carpool lanes, newspaper racks, snack boxes, donation boxes, and restaurant dining all have something to do with *keeping your word*. So does everything you do in the service you render your customer. When you make a promise to a customer, the honor system obliges you to keep your word. Police officers catch carpool lane scofflaws, fellow workers turn in people who take snacks without paying, and restaurants go after people who skip paying their bill. Your customers know when you fail to keep your word. Or perhaps that should be your ex-customers know it.

The Benefit of the Doubt

The honor system is indeed a *system*. It includes not just you, but everyone in your proximity. It allows you to include your customers in the same system. There are many obvious ways in which you can trust your customers to be players in your honor system. You can reserve an item by phone on customers' assurances that they'll pick it up later in the day. You can adjust a return policy, extend a discount past the expired date for valued customers, stay late to help a customer who promises to come in, or validate the parking of a customer who has not purchased anything. Each act of goodwill draws your customer into a mutual system of trust. As that mutual trust grows, so does the strength of your relationship.

Years of experience with honor systems prove that people can be trusted to do the right thing when they are given the opportunity. But when trust is breached or liberties taken, people conclude that their trust has been misplaced. Getting that trust back is a lot more difficult than earning it in the first place. So, if you live by the ethical standards, common sense, and professional courtesy that are part of the honor system, you can earn the trust that comes when people know they can depend on you. Respecting the honor system makes you feel good about yourself, and it establishes in your customers' mind that you are a person they want to do business with.

An Orchestrated Effort

Develop your teamwork.

Much of what you do as a customer service representative is done in conjunction with other professionals with the intention of creating a smoothly running work environment. When you and your colleagues do this successfully, you not only make your job easier, but it also makes you a viable and cooperative partner in commerce.

Customers do not pay a great deal of consideration to your efforts to work well with your co-workers or business professionals. Your networking efforts are done behind the scenes, and they are often transparent to outsiders. The end result, though, is a comfortable experience for the customer.

The ability to work in concert with others is important if you expect to enjoy a successful work day. Throughout the day, you may find yourself working with suppliers, sales associates, receptionists, delivery personnel, and other professionals. Each interaction affects how smooth-running your work day is.

A Symphony of Success

To get a sense of what working cooperatively with other professionals is like, consider the example of a symphony orchestra. Within the structure of a symphony orchestra are dozens of very accomplished, well-trained, and disciplined professional musicians. Each has studied and rehearsed his or her craft to the point of being recognized by their instructors and peers.

Individual musicians often sacrifice a great deal both personally and financially to be a member of the orchestra. Each musician takes pride in his or her accomplishments and talent. But each also recognizes that individual talent alone cannot create the symphony orchestra.

This unforgettable sound is created when experienced and talented individuals all work in concert with one another under the direction of the musical conductor. The conductor directs the talent. He or she works diligently to orchestrate the musicians together to create the distinctive symphonic sound.

Practice Makes Perfect

As an employee, it's easy to think of yourself as a self-contained professional who does not need anyone else to perform your job. In retail sales, there are security devices, credit card machines, register supplies, supervisor support, and a variety of aids to help you perform your duties. The self-employed can rely on all the outside professionals who supply support and direction. And it's easy to take all these things for granted. The truth is, though, you need other professionals, and they need you. Once you apply the concepts of synergy and teamwork to your day-to-day routines, you will discover that you have a great effect on the successful outcomes of your workday.

Think of yourself as the soloist who performs the first movement of a classical concerto. It might be beautiful and incredibly moving, but without the accompaniment of the orchestra, it will simply be a performance taken out of context. The other instruments and the harmonic blends to the musical score create the piece as a finished product.

The same holds true for your actions as an individual employee. When you work handedly with other professionals, you complete the musical score. At work and elsewhere, all things need to work in harmony with one another. There may not be a conductor to lead the way. But you may not need one. A pro-active approach may be the catalyst to move your career with the company forward.

A Symphonic Environment

Just imagine what it would be like if all customer service representatives were to adopt this same cooperative concept. We are all accomplished, learned, talented, and dedicated professionals who can stand on our own. But by working in unison under the direction of a conductor, everyone's individual talents come together in a harmonious blend of unrivalled symphonic sound.

It really is not difficult to do. Many professionals are already doing it by devoting themselves seriously to their employer and their co-workers. It takes a concerted effort by many to create a workplace symphony. It is only pride that stands in the way. A go-it-alone approach or an unwillingness to allow a conductor to orchestrate the talents will stymie the progressive efforts of other workers. Don't let that obstruction be you!

four

YOU Are the Final Piece of the Puzzle!

Before you can make it "all about them," take a step back and look at the bigger picture. How important are you in the overall structure of your company? The answer is: more important than you might think! Your contribution at each customer encounter carries a tremendous responsibility. Nearly everything is riding on you and your ability to represent the company, its products, and services. This affects word-of-mouth referrals and the overall reputation of the business.

If it sounds like a heavy cross to bear, well...it is! But if you are successful in carrying this burden, you will prove your value to your employer. With that will come more money, better reviews, promotions, greater acceptance, and additional steps up the ladder to success.

Take a good look around you. Examine everything as it relates to the business you represent. If there are products on the shelf, your job is to get them into the customers' hands. If you are in the service or hospitality industry, your job is to be informative and helpful to each customer. This will maximize their experience. You are the final piece of the puzzle to satisfy every customer.

Let's look a little deeper. Let's empty the box and place all the puzzle pieces on the table. To put this puzzle together, you need look at everything that goes into the product and service you offer. In retail sales, each product begins with research, design, and development. Hundreds of hours are spent to create a prototype for each product. In larger companies, a team of individuals usually look closely at a products usability, safety, practicality, effectiveness, and durability.

Once the prototype is developed, the product goes through a series of rigorous tests to establish its viability. From there, it's on to the factory, where many workers assemble the product for distribution. Behind the scenes is the acquisition of the materials needed to assemble the product. These must be purchased in large quantities so that each product is consistent in quality, workmanship, and construction.

After the final product is assembled, it must be packaged. Product packaging is an art form in itself. Here again, a team of people, including; marketing and advertising specialists, graphic artists, and designers (among others) have worked to create an appealing package that will draw the attention of consumers.

Before the finished product leaves the factory, a team of marketing and advertising specialists have come together to create an extensive advertising campaign to build anticipation and interest for the product. Meanwhile, other professionals in television, radio, or print media have begun working on the advertisements that will reach out to the public. As consumer interest grows, so does the demand for the product.

By this time hundreds of people may be involved with the product. And the product has not even left the factory yet. It still needs to be distributed. Before it has been delivered to your business, a distribution team has mapped out the logistics, manner, and costs of freight to ensure that the product reaches its final destination. At last the product is in front of you, and only now can you deliver the kind of customer service that sells the item.

Before you start, take a look around you. What you will see is a business that has gone through its own version of product design and development. It started with a vision, a location, an investment, and a business plan. The owner has worked tirelessly to hire and train a staff of people who will work in the company's best interests and help it establish a reputation that continues to attract customers. The business has been marketed and advertised locally to get and keep its name and reputation before the public. The owner has worked with suppliers and other outside services to maintain everything that you see around you. Policies, procedures, training, and the on-going review of daily operations come together to create this moment.

Everything is in place. The doors are finally open for business. Now it is your opportunity to shine. YOU are the final piece of this puzzle! The company, the product, and the customer intersect right where you are standing. The only thing that stands between you and the sale of the product is your ability to give great customer service! If you are successful, the transaction will be completed, and everyone who has worked so hard to bring the product to market will benefit from your efforts. And so will your customer!

There's also a trickledown effect that works from the point of sale back to the beginning of the product's inception. When your company places another order to replenish its inventory of product, it creates job security for hundreds of people involved with this product. Many people depend on you and your ability to deliver great customer service. You are the point of contact where this product reaches its final destination. Without you, there is no sale. And that's why your job is so important.

It works the same way in the service industry. Substitute products for equipment and supplies. The same careful and rigorous development, packaging, and distribution go into every item that is used. The end result is an effort that is put forth and made possible by many people.

In the hospitality industry, many factors contribute to customer satisfaction. If you work in a hotel, just take a look around at everything that surrounds you. Whether you are in the lobby, the elevator, the restaurant, the business center, or the fitness room, a long list of people have created the environment where you work and deal with customers.

Only one person can make or break the experience for your customer. That person is you! So never show up at work and simply go through the motions. Every person responsible for the delivery of a product or service is a piece of the big puzzle. So many people have painstakingly placed each piece together to create a picture of the perfect transaction. If one piece is lost or misplaced, the puzzle is incomplete. When the final piece of the puzzle—*you*—is inserted, the transaction is complete. The customer is satisfied and the hard work of everyone is finally realized. Thanks to you!

About the Author

Before his teen years were over, Larry William Dietsch had worked a variety of retail positions. By the time he was a young adult, he had several years' experience in various retail outlets. After studying accounting in college, he entered the business world, where he enjoyed a successful tenure at the Space Division of the Rockwell International Corporation.

In 1989, he moved to Northern Nevada and one day, walked into a radio station. What began as a simple inquiry turned into an internship as a radio broadcaster and a new profession. Under his new air name, Larry Williams, he began a broadcasting career that quickly opened doors to opportunity. He hosted a successful daily radio show; he made personal appearances throughout the community; he wrote articles and interviewed celebrities for numerous newspapers and magazines; and he served as a professional Master of Ceremonies for corporate and private events.

Eventually, he began a successful service business in the wedding industry. He continued to write extensively for the retail, service, and hospitality industries in which he was involved. Through his leadership, educational offerings, and public speaking, Larry Williams set a standard for customer service that became recognized and emulated regionally and nationally.

Meanwhile, he continued to pour himself into research and education. A successful businessman, journalist, broadcaster, and public speaker, Williams developed fresh, innovative, and cutting-edge techniques that earned him the respect of his peers and the appreciation of a grateful industry.

Williams remained active in community projects and regional and national causes. In 2006, the American Disc Jockey Association awarded him the prestigious ADJA Michael Butler Humanitarian Award for his efforts in the wake of the Hurricane Katrina disaster.

His greatest reward came in 2009. Touched early in his radio career by the story of an eleven-year-old girl who was kidnapped while walking to the school bus stop, he wrote a song that became the "official" song of the search effort. In 2009, Williams joined the worldwide celebration for Jaycee Lee Dugard, who was found alive and reunited with her family after eighteen years of captivity. To this day, the song "Jaycee Lee" that he wrote in 1991 is one of the proudest accomplishments in his life and career.

Today, Larry Williams remains passionate about touching and improving the lives of others. It is a recurring theme at his home, which he shares with his wife, Selly, and their children, Jenny and Joey. *Always strive to achieve a harmonious balance of family, work, and self improvement!* has become Williams' personal byline.

What Readers Are Saying

Finally, a book on customer service that dares to "tell it like it is." It is practical, "time tested" and edgy... the perfect tutorial for novices, seasoned professionals, or anyone interested in achieving stellar customer relationships and outcomes.

— Kerry L. Miller, City Manager, Folsom, CA

Basic and sensible concepts are far from being practiced in customer service today. By bringing the focus back to the fundamentals of quality, Larry Williams is helping to correct this in a highly effective manner.

— Peter Merry, Author of *The Best Wedding Reception Ever!*

Down to earth, simple, understandable customer service basics presented comprehensively. A great tool for owners and managers as well as for front line employees who want to excel and advance.

— Bill Chernock , Executive Director, Carson Valley Chamber of Commerce and Visitors Authority

When you are involved in community broadcasting for more than four decades, you see a lot of people fake their way through customer service. This book is the real deal. It will teach everyone who reads it the right way to treat customers.

— Lloyd Higuera, Manager, Douglas County Community Access Television

It is so refreshing to see a book that addresses real-life conditions in the retail industry. Customer Service A to Z *details all the things I want my employees to know and understand about interacting with customers.*

— Mark Bell, Owner, Reno Gallery of Furniture

Customer Service A to Z *brings to mind the lessons of childhood, and these fundamentals still apply in adulthood. Learn these lessons well and begin your journey to customer service excellence!*

— Lynn Jackson and Bill Capodagli, coauthors *The Disney Way, The Disney Way Fieldbook* and *Innovate the Pixar Way*

Seminars • Webinars • Book Signings

Author Larry Williams is available for a variety of personal appearances. If your group, organization, conference or business is looking for a dynamic presentation on customer service, Larry Williams would welcome the opportunity to bring this topic "to life" in a manner that will motivate your attendees.

More and more national conferences are beginning to see the benefit of customer service-related seminars and the direct relationship they have to the sales process. Larry Williams will outline the steps necessary not only to increase sales, profits, and word-of-mouth referrals, but also to establish a model that will ensure you have satisfied customers for life!

The entire seminar was well-paced, informative and enjoyable! And the ending was inspirational! Talk about closing with a bang! Larry Williams brought the house down and was the only speaker to receive a standing ovation for the entire conference! WOW!!!

— Scott Faver, National Entertainer and Motivational Speaker

Case Sales: When you purchase *Customer Service A to Z* by the case, you can receive a unit price that represents more than a 50% savings.

Customer Service A to Z Award: This "Award of Excellence", presented at each public appearance at no charge, will recognize the merits of outstanding customer service for one of your attendees.

For contact information and social media links:
www.CustomerServiceAtoZ.com